John Fraser, Otto Peltzer

The moralist and the theatre

John Fraser, Otto Peltzer

The moralist and the theatre

ISBN/EAN: 9783337303693

Printed in Europe, USA, Canada, Australia, Japan

Cover: Foto ©Andreas Hilbeck / pixelio.de

More available books at **www.hansebooks.com**

THE

MORALIST AND THE THEATRE

A SERIES OF ARTICLES
WHICH ORIGINALLY APPEARED IN "MUSIC AND DRAMA,"
EMBRACING A BRIEF

HISTORY OF THE STAGE,

ITS RELATION TO THE

CHURCH,

ITS INFLUENCE, ITS PRESENT CONDITION AND NEEDED REFORM.

BY

OTTO PELTZER.

TRANSLATOR OF "URIEL ACOSTA," A TRAGEDY IN FIVE ACTS; "THE ERL-KING'S DAUGHTER," A
DRAMATIC BALLAD; AND "THE LORD'S PRAYER OF MASONRY," ETC.

WITH A CRITICISM BY

JOHN FRASER. A. M.

LATE PROFESSOR OF ENGLISH LITERATURE, CHICAGO UNIVERSITY; DRAMATIC AND ART CRITIC FOR
THE "CHICAGO TRIBUNE," "GLASGOW HERALD," AND "IRISH TIMES,"

ON A BIBLICAL DRAMA ENTITLED

"MOSES AND PHARAOH."

CHICAGO:

PUBLISHED BY DONALD FRASER & SONS,

1887.

NEW OPERA HOUSE, PARIS.

PREFACE.

CHICAGO, DECEMBER, 1886.

OTTO PELTZER, Esq.,

Dear Sir:

Your articles on the Theatre, which appeared
last winter in "*Music and Drama*," have been read with great interest by many who have the welfare of the Theatre and the Drama at
heart. At the special request of a number of them, who are anxious
to have your articles preserved in more permanent form, we wish to
ask if you mean to have them published in book form? If so, we
desire to secure the right of publication. In doing this we would like
to add to your articles an elaborate criticism of the late Prof. John
Fraser, which we feel assured would prove of interest to the same
class of readers.

Yours truly,

DONALD FRASER & SONS.

CHICAGO, DECEMBER, 1886.

MESSRS. DONALD FRASER & SONS,

Dear Sirs:

Your letter is before me. It stands to reason
that the object for which the articles to which you refer were originally prepared by me will be the better served by the use you propose
to make of them.

As to the articles themselves it will be hardly necessary for me to
make excuses for any short-comings in their aim or for the occasional
repetitions of thought, as they were written from time to time for use

in a weekly paper, and not for publication in book form. Their purpose to arouse an interest in the better drama and purer stage is apparent. By the addition of an article from the pen of Prof. John Fraser, I can only feel honored, as I am satisfied that such an article can not be antagonistic to the Theatre and the Drama.

The sphere of the Theatre should be wide enough and the aim of the Drama high enough to embrace the great truths and the sound morals of life. Truth and morality must be taught consistently and uniformly everywhere. Upon the stage and in the public prints as in the homes, the schools and churches of a people, or else all the good work of the latter is soon nullified by the evil influences of the first.

The popularity of the theatre must be utilized to cultivate the deep and subtle distinctions between right and wrong and thereby continually strengthen its patrons against the evil inclinings of their grosser natures.

Truth and morality must be the pillars of all public institutions so that they may teach us constantly the greatest of all lessons—how to live.

Very Respectfully Yours,

OTTO PELTZER.

CONTENTS.

LIST OF ILLUSTRATIONS.

The Globe Theatre, London.
Erected 1594.

The Paris Garden Theatre, London.
Erected prior to 1544.

The Fortune Theatre, London.
Erected 1599.

THE CHURCH AND THE THEATRE.

AN ARGUMENT.

"Reform it altogether."—Hamlet.

In the title to this argument the church is placed first, because the argument itself is principally addressed to the thoughtful followers of that institution.

These are terrible times—savage times—times lacking every vestige of respect for honesty and manliness. ·Virility is at a discount, flabby æstheticism is mistaken for refinement, delicate points of honor are met with derision, trusts are broken, and faith is wanting in every station. Slum journalism, vilely-illustrated prints and the dime novel, like immoral epidemics, are sapping the morals of our youth. Money, money, seems to be the sole aim of all our struggles.

What will be the outcome of this? Where in all this world is the regenerating power to start from? This is the unsolved problem of the day.

There are certain duties which man so sacredly owes to his fellow-beings and to the human race which is to succeed him, that no amount of sophistry will excuse or justify their neglect. One of these duties is that no matter how lowly his station or sphere in life, he must at all times lend, at least, his moral support and encouragement, and under certain conditions and circumstances, render active or pecuniary aid to the correction, reformation or banishment of existing evils, prejudices and social wrongs. As to what constitute the latter, and what will work their correction or banishment, he must use his own best judgment, nor ever close his ears to the reasoning and respectful suggestions of others, who may differ with him at times as to the methods and means for reformation.

Every member of cosmopolitan society, who respects religion, while he is above the narrow views of fanaticism, and who, at the same time, has given any thought to the proper sphere of the theatre, will be readily induced to join in the hope, that before long the last vestige of prejudice against the theatre, as an institution, shall have been completely rooted out amongst those who denominate themselves christians.

This is in all seriousness "a consummation devoutly to be wished." It is to be hoped that every practical christian, desirous of upholding and spreading the moral teachings of his faith, may be persuaded to see, that it is a dangerous policy to continually weaken his own cause by injudicious, uncalled for and really useless attacks upon the legitimate entertainments that have sprung from the very church itself in its earliest time.

The church is not expected to hold out the hand of fellowship to the theatre at once, but only as the latter's own special efforts for its serious improvement shall warrant. It is not even essential that "the middle wall of partition" which Professor Blackie, the learned Greek scholar of Edinburgh University, says "has been artificially raised in England between the pulpit and the stage," shall be completely broken down. Each of these two institutions has its peculiar field of harmonious usefulness the same as the church and the school.

But as this same learned Professor says "Unless the God of nature and the God of the Bible be two different deities—which I think Bishop Butler proved triumphantly they are not, then the drama is fundamentally from God as much as the sermon, and the stage is a divine institution no less than the pulpit."

A critic of recognized ability in England in a recent number of a London monthly says, "Between church and stage there should be no hostility, but unfortunately there has been what we believe is only an apparent hostility entirely created and fostered by the wanton attacks on the stage made by members of the clergy, who can not recognize the fact that the noblest of human amusements has always sought alliance and not war with the noblest principles of religion."

Can the thoughtful christian be induced to abandon his futile opposition to an institution which, in its proper condition in one form or another, has in its early days been a strong moral ally of church and state, and has deservedly enjoyed the support and admiration of all ages the world over?

This is a serious question of the greatest importance to both the church and the theatre, and therefore to the morals of our land.

It is not intended here to defend the occasional individual errors of
the disciples of the stage any more than it is proposed to assail the
church for the not infrequent frailties of men in the pulpit and their followers.

Let those among them both, who fall by the wayside, answer for
their errors the same as the rest of mortals.

Most broad-minded men, not professing christianity, accord a ready
respect to those who honestly espouse its cause as well as to the theatre,
as the latter is a sort of universal church of humanity where good is
shown and where evil is exposed in bold colors. The great trouble,
however, is that broad-mindedness toward those who fearlessly differ
with him has seldom been a striking characteristic of the orthodox
christian. If the theatre is debased, reform it. Do not attempt to destroy it, for man will not be without it. The high offices of the pulpit
have been, and are now, frequently abused. That is no justification
for the destruction of the church, with its great teachings.

It was St. Paul who said to the Romans, "Let us cast off the work
of darkness, and put on the armor of light." Let the christian bear in
mind that the world ever advances in one direction or another, but
never toward the darkness of fanaticism and bigotry. Let him bear in
mind that violent and indiscriminate attacks by church followers upon
so popular an institution as the theatre, with a view to working its ultimate destruction, will not be tolerated, but will engender the hostility
of the institution attacked and arouse its supporters with equal violence against the church, and it then becomes a serious question which
of the two will suffer most.

The theatre has a foundation as deep, as old, as firm and solid
as the church. It is an institution that has openly at all times enjoyed
the support and respect of the greatest and the best the world ever
produced. The anchors of the stage and its literature are cast way
down into the very hearts of the people. Those who indiscriminately
invoke divine judgment against the stage and its literature, forget that
every book we read, unto the very Bible itself, is but a drama, pictur-
ing to our mind's eye, through its voiceless leaves, the scenes and incidents which distance and lapse of time prevent our seeing and hear-
ing as a reality.

The Bible, from Genesis to the Revelation, is but a series of
dramas. There is fiction in the story of the prodigal son. There is
romance in the life of Rachel. There is poetry and music in the
songs of Miriam. There is poetry of motion in the wild dancing of

David before the daughters of Saul. There is heroism in the death of Samson. There is melodrama in the career of Moses. There is poetic justice in the destruction of Pharaoh in the Red sea, and there is the most sublime tragedy in the life and the crucifixion of the Saviour. .

Man and woman are the embodiment of dramatic acting, from the cradle to the final retirement from the stage of this world.

The restless babe is at once fascinated, and its pitiful cries are readily quieted by the playful mimicry, the smiling face and the tuneful voice of the mother. She is the first actress on the stage of life who appears to that little one. She turns the little weeping face into a mirror of smiles, in accordance with her ability to play her part.

The chubby girl will "act" the part of mother to her doll in a few years, and the little mischievous boy will imitate the peculiarities of those older than himself. His most popular games are those in which he plays the part of somebody else. The lessons in declamation have more attraction in school than the lessons in arithmetic.

The author who, as the better and more consummate character delineator, can command his words and rivet our attention so as to bring us nearest to the objects of his writings, is always the most forcible and interesting. The minister who, in the pulpit, can most perfectly, by word and gesture, delineate sufferings, death and the final triumph of life, has ever been the most popular one.

What constitutes the more successful doctor, lawyer, merchant, clerk, or salesman, who in their branch of business or profession come into direct contact with the general public? Nine cases out of ten, the better and more natural any of these "act" their "parts" for which they are "cast" in the great "drama of life," the greater will be their success and reward.

Why is life in the workshop or the household to many men and women almost too monotonous to endure? Because there they have only the opportunity to use their minds and bodies to play the little part of "self."

Civilization, in its most perfect form, so far as it concerns social intercourse between humankind, is "acting." The more honest and sincere, the more refined and artistic, the more natural and the less artificial this "acting" is, the more perfect is this form of civilization.

Take a person in every-day life with a peculiar tone of voice, with extremely eccentric mannerisms, with an awkward gait, and with an obtrusive and meddlesome disposition, and everybody will surely vote him an intolerable nuisance. But let another mimic him on or off the stage in all these peculiarlities and characteristics, and it will at once interest and amuse. Find a couple married or unmarried, with their young hearts full of ardent love and true feeling, and let them expose their natural affection before their friends in the parlor, and they will soon find themselves deserted as spooney simpletons. Yet *Romeo* and *Juliet* and *Claude* and *Pauline* are nightly applauded for simulating the same feelings on the stage.

Men and women will pass squalor and hunger in rags upon the streets a hundred times a day without so much as turning about, unless hunger and rags clutch their beaver overcoats and sealskin sacques; and yet these same beaver overcoats and sealskin sacques will weep copious tears at this same hunger and squalor "acted on the boards." There are thousands of noble men and women in our midst whose thoughts and actions deserve favorable recognition; but we do not know *Hamlet, Parthenia, Camille, Lea Henderson, Osip, Master Walter, John Strebelow, Virginius, Lanciotto* and the heroes at our side, unless there is an orchestra between us and a row of glaring lights thrown upon them.

The poet says that all the world is a stage, and the men and women are only players, but he forgot to tell us that, to be applauded, they must exhibit themselves under the direction of an experienced stage manager. This has led to systematically-arranged dramas or plays, or whatever they may be called. The more perfect and complete these representations and their surroundings in the theatre are, the more popular they ever have been, and ever will be.

The drama, properly comprehended, has in it a higher purpose than the mere narration of bare facts. It is life's realities placed before us in their most interesting and idealized form, clothed in their best garb, *stripped of all their vulgar features*, brought vividly to our conception for our entertainment and for our instruction through the agency of high art and stage artifice.

The drama, properly represented in the theatre by those who make it a study, should no more come under the ban of the high-minded christian and moralist than should that which is presented to us through books, the lecture-room or in the pulpit. Why should it be more questionable, enacted in an appropriate and a picturesque garb by those to the purpose drilled, than that recited by the frequently discordant voices and with the awkward gesture of the rostrum, or that hidden in the less interesting pages of fiction or history?

It must be confessed with sorrow and humiliation, that there is much room for argument against a certain class of productions on the stage of to-day which do not abound in good to those who witness them—productions in which art is sacrificed to questionable show and in which vice does not even care to wear a mask. It is to be regretted that, like the sensational scandal-and-criminal-columns of the daily papers, these exhibitions are intensely gratifying to a certain class of patrons of the theatre. Their tone, however, as well as their temperament and their method, bears no more relation to dramatic art than slum journalism to literature. The jargon of the swamp, the debasing lingo of the police reporter, the abounding epithet of tap room frequenters, the colloquialisms of the street arabs will come trippingly from the pen of these play-makers. Horrors intensified, grossness exaggerated, modern barbarity, the doings of swindlers, drunkards, beggars, thieves, the lowest form of degradation, scenes in the gambling hells and prisons, the brutalities of the lunatic asylum, accidents, explosions and mangled limbs, are their leading features.

Plays with convicts for heroes; with plots made up of impossibilities and exaggerations, until the whole is nauseating to the most ordinary intelligence, give no instruction—they are monstrosities that teach no lesson. They positively poison the minds of a young generation.

Plays of this character in times gone by were performed, but until within the last few years their production was confined to the lowest grade of the London, Paris and New York play-houses that would not be listed in the roster of respectable theatres.

The doors of the proudest dramatic temples are open to them to-day in our glorious country, and the scourge is stalking through the land. Formerly their authors preferred to be unknown, or else they were notorious. To-day they are brazen-faced men of distinction. This is sad. Besides this, theatrical management has so largely fallen into the hands of speculating adventurers, that the few remaining pillars of the old school of actor-managers exercise but little or no influence in the choice of "attractions." These speculating adventurers are dishonoring the field of dramatic management; as the compilers of vicious plays are dishonoring the field of dramatic literature. Their productions make us unduly familiar with bludgeons, with coarse words, with stale wit and sickening sights. They deaden us to sorrow that ought to sadden us. They do not make us better. They debase those who look upon them. That they flourish is less the fault of the theatre than the fault of the vitiated and morbid taste of those who rush to witness them.

Let every high-minded and intelligent man or woman, be he or she christian or unbeliever, refuse to patronize them, and they will soon disappear from the places they now usurp.

Their banishment cannot be accomplished, however, by crying against the theatre as an institution, by warring upon it for its destruction.

The world will no more exist hereafter without the stage than it has heretofore. Man can no more live without the light of the drama than vegetation can flourish without the light of the sun. The electric light of the present is better than the tallow dip of the past, but we must also have the light of the sun in all its glorious brightness. We must have the theatre and the drama with all its refining influences, with all its power to better our thoughts and actions.

Those gifted by the Creator with minds, with souls, with hearts and brains, cannot all walk the earth with their eyes cast upon the ground, and with their bodies clothed in sack-cloth and ashes. That would turn this world into an abode of mourning, and make life irksome toil to millions. We must have diversion, such as will give relief from toil, and make us fit for higher and nobler uses.

Is it proper, is it just, is it reasonable to consider the only ideal of life, pure and simple, to be abnegation and ascetic self-repression? Is it not more humane and reasonable and god-like to consider fulfilment, harmonic exaltation and completeness of being and function the true ideal of life? It would certainly appear that the fulfilment of all the normal offices of our nature in their co-ordinate plenitude of power cannot offend our Creator. Is it not a narrow and morbid superstition to look upon complete self-sacrifice as the only means of salvation. Are not fanatical ferocity, sentimental melancholy, dismal gloom and narrow mechanical formalism and cant really vices of the church, and are these vices of the church not indirectly responsible for such frivolity, reckless gaiety, conviviality and voluptuousness in the theatre.

If this is the age of realism on the stage, of mechanical effects, of scenic display, let the advance that has been made in this direction be utilized upon a better grade of dramatic literature, instead of to the latter's entire exclusion. The world must have ideal, purified heroes, above the common level, to be admired, to be held up before the young mind as models for emulation. The dramatists can create them from among the great men and women of the past, and let them tread the stage as flesh and blood, and the noble thoughts and actions of the dead will be applauded and emulated by the living when seen in the bright surroundings of the theatre.

The heroes of ancient and modern history, the rulers of nations, the reformers, the statesmen, the patriots and the warriors can live their days over again before our eyes, on the stage. The patron of the theatre hears their voices as they soliloquize, he sees them draped in their classic togas and robes of virility; he follows them through their illustrious lives ; he admires their valor on the battle-field or their wisdom and oratory in the forum, and he mourns over the end of their greatness as the curtain of their lives goes down. He sees with his own eyes and hears with his own ears how posterity honors the great and good of the past, and this will spur him on to noble actions.

The stage can teach the theatre-goer to hate those who were wicked, to sympathize with those who were unfortunate, and to love and honor those who were grand and good.

As the theatre aims directly to entertain—it can aim indirectly to teach, persuade and impress. It can do the latter much better than any other educational institution, because of the pleased condition of the soul, induced by the success of the first, and because it does it without the often repulsive severity of those who claim the task of moral guidance as their professional office.

The sailor on the high sea, the laborer on the docks, the seamstress toiling away in a loft or factory, the mechanic at the work-bench, the merchant hidden among his goods, the professional man plucking out his brains in his office—all alike can study these living lessons, after hours of duty—in the theatre to their delight and recreation. Thus they become intimate with the great enactors of the world's history, of whom otherwise they would have known nothing. At the theatre they can shake hands with them across the foot-lights, during hours that might otherwise be wasted in idleness or dissipation.

The drama as it might and would be, if it were properly encouraged by those who now injudiciously cry against it, teaches lessons which neither youth nor manhood ever forgets. The lessons inspire the inquiring mind, and they lead him to the study and to the enlargement of his limited knowledge on the foundation of these living instructions. The drama is capable of teaching a religion that bears not only on the sinfulness of sin, but also on the rascality of lying, of stealing, of hypocrisy, and of all the petty vices in their endless varieties. It is an institution of learning where men and women may acquire knowledge, which in their conditions and circumstances, unhappily, were denied them in their youth.

In older countries the stage has always been regarded, and has been wisely used by those in high places, as a friendly ally to the church and the state. Greece had no more respected teachers of whatever it honored and encouraged than its great tragedians. Racine and Corneille have been the pride, and Moliere has been the moral guide of France. As for Schiller, Goethe, and the greatest of them all, the immortal Shakespeare, what have they not all done in imparting lofty sentiments to the world!

In proportion to its opportunities, the theatre has at all times exercised a greater influence in educating the masses than any other institution. The mimic scenes upon the stage can hold the most vicious rabble spell-bound; it can subdue the unbridled passions of a mob and move the most illiterate to tears. The appeals of the stage to the senses are more direct and potent than those of any other educational method.

Whatever most perfects men and women, and imparts to them the accomplishments and arts most admired, can be employed there. Oratory, poetry, song, sculpture, music, painting and literature are there represented in living forms and at their best. Is it wrong to enjoy them beneath the roof of a theatre? Whatever is refined in manners, loftiest in principle and heroic in character can be illustrated on the stage more completely and effectively than anywhere else. Is it wrong to admire these characteristics, illustrated in living lessons on the stage?

If the liberal-minded followers of the church and the serious moralists are honest in their desire for effective reform and wish to act with reason and judgment, they should call to their aid the only ally of strength and influence among the masses—the theatre.

Its undeniable power has often been made use of most effectively by the monarchs of the old world, for purposes of their own. At their instigation plays have been written and their success fostered by subsidies and otherwise—plays which have averted or precipitated conflicts within their realms, and thus either given direct security to their thrones, or brought about the destruction of conflicting elements. The masses of their subjects have been educated in doctrines, and principles have been promulgated, leading either to peace or war, as occasion demanded. Again, authors like Moliere, Hugo, Dumas, Sardou and others, have always effectively used the theatre for the promulgation of their pet hobbies.

The theatres of Germany have done more, years ago, to allay the old prejudice against the Jews than all other influences combined. The plays which were written with such purposes in view are known in the dramatic literature of Germany under the distinctive classification of *tendency dramas*, a classification altogether unknown in this country and in England. It is an uncultivated field here, so far. Why not try its power for the moral reform of our growing generation? Lessons in morality, in manliness, nobleness, honor and true valor, made interesting by the art of the dramatist, and illustrated on the stage by the art of acting, the whole surrounded by the modern improvements in legitimate stage representation, will always improve the mind, stir the soul, touch the heart, and move the listener to a purer life. Let the efforts in this direction of capable pens and willing managers meet with the effective support, with the solid encouragement, and the steady patronage of the liberal christian and the sensible moralist, and the undeniable power of the stage for good, will soon be felt all over the land.

The Rev. Dr. Mark Trafton, of Boston, a well-known Methodist of pronounced views, recently appeared at a ministers' meeting and made a very interesting plea for non-church-goers. He took the ground that the seeming falling off in attendance on Protestant churches in the cities was due largely to the increase of the Catholic population and the increase also of Jews. The rapid growth of suburban cities, the bedrooms of Boston, also took away thousands of church-goers. The speaker said high pew-rents were a bar to large congregations, and cited Tremont temple and the People's Church (both free) to prove his assertion. "Let me start out now to worship God. We come to the church door—I am saying what took place exactly—we see plenty of seats vacant. In the gallery you see four young people talking and laughing. Suddenly the organ starts, and then as suddenly the four grow solemn, jump up, and begin to squall. They sing a hymn you never heard before. You can't sing with them. Call that singing God's praise! It is not only folly, but blasphemy. You've no business to introduce such trash and call it devotion. Well, it was over; and then the man read the bible [here the speaker read in imitation in a quick, monotonous, low, and sing-song way a passage from the scriptures]. There is a way to read the scriptures by which you can fix the attention of the people. There is too much caste in our churches. What we want is the real, old-fashioned sociability. That will reach the people." These are some of the errors of the church as depicted by one of its own disciples.

The Rev. Mr. Greene, of Chicago, took occasion to say in his fare well sermon to his congregation. "You have no quicker method of determining the spirit of life than by a single glance at its recreations. Look at the stage then, by way of illustration. I enjoy the drama; I always have; I always will, I suppose. The magnificent plays of Shakespeare—the tragic working out of history in mimic reproduction; the enjoyable presentation of comedy—all these may be instructive and recreative. But look at the stage to-day. Four-fifths of the current drama is popular by force of its nastiness. The dressing up of sin, the depicting of vice, the very dialogue sparkling with shafts of wit whose light is fired by hell. What does it signify? That drama is evil? By no means! It merely voices the popular taste, that craves nastiness. It draws better than anything else." So thinks a divine of the drama.

Why will the church follower and the moralist close their eyes and ears to the truth of these undeniable facts, and enforce strife against the theatre instead of making a proper effort for its reform.

The church unquestionably has lost much of the influence it wielded many years ago over the great body of the people of any country. There has been quite a reaction against the once favorite idea that truth, honor and goodness is confined to its folds only. Men of the world have found that virtue and right is by no means universal among the followers of the church. Elijah found, when lying under the juniper tree wishing to die, believing that he was the only one who served the true God, that there were five thousand priests in Israel who had not bowed their knees to Baal. It is a weakness of the church to cling to creed—it is its mistake to insist upon conforming all opinions to its own narrow standard. We know that many are saved by the church —saved from much sin even in these times.

The church has been a great power in this world, but are the doctrines of it deep enough to defy the storms of this age of reason?

Does its faithful army feel strong enough to pitch its tents for a war of destruction against the theatre, with its hold upon the hearts of the people, in these days of freedom of thought? Does the church dare to jeopardize its future and the morals of the people in the hours that lead the world away from old dogmatic theories? Behold the daily-increasing and well-disciplined army of free-thinkers, who openly proclaim christianity a failure.

The free-thinkers of the country, men well meaning and honorable citizens, who have just concluded a convention at Albany, N. Y., have given out a declaration of principles and aims. The following extract from their resolves fully indicates the temper of the gathering:

"That, taking our stand on the fundamental American doctrine of the separation of church and state, we demand in the interests of liberty, equal rights and secular government, that such separation of church and state should be completed: (a) By the appeal of all laws exempting church and ecclesiastical property from taxation. (b) By the prohibition by law of the appropriation of public money for the support of or use by institutions under the management and influence of sectarian denominations. (c) By the repeal of all laws compelling the observance of any day as a Sabbath or holy day, or enforcing the observance of any day as a Sabbath or holy day, or enforcing the payment of legislative chaplaincies, or of establishing special religious days to be observed by public authority. We therefore call upon our fellow-citizens, irrespective of their religious opinions, to aid us in obtaining these simple requirements of justice.

"That the object of free thought is to extend the benign influence of science, to cultivate the spirit of fraternity, to aid in the triumph of peace, to remove brute force, and to inaugurate a government which shall express the moral power of an enlightened reason. To these ends we recommend: (a) That liberal and secular societies should be formed for social education and recreative purposes. (b) That free-thought and secular halls, libraries and reading rooms should be built or obtained, and that suitable lecturers and teachers should be employed wherever possible, in the several counties of our state.

"That it is time for liberal and secular societies to take the place of churches and priests in the social recognition and celebration of those great events of human life—birth, marriage and death.

"That inasmuch as government rests upon the consent of the governed, equality recognizes no distinction of sex, and that woman's complete inclusion into a common participation with man of the knowledge of the uses and the enjoyments of this earth is her legitimate position.

"That theology, in accounting for toil as a curse and in proclaiming riches as a snare, has unhappily confused the relations of labor and capital, and that human equality demand that the industry which creates the wealth of the world should enjoy a fair distribution of its benefits." These are the promulgations of "free thought."

Is the influence of such a movement to be constantly undervalued?

Let the christian warrior look well to his weapons. Let him look well to the stores of his ammunition before continuing longer upon a war path, the end of which he has every reason to fear. Upon calm consideration he will find it the better part of wisdom to change his line of battle and to make common cause with the honest friends of the theatre for a brave fight against the great evils of the day at which we all stand appalled.

That there are followers of the church whose sound judgment, whose broadness of vision, and whose spirit of fairness and liberality prompts them to boldly. concede to the theatre the great influences here accorded to it, is amply proved by the following article, taken from the columns of a daily paper.

"CRIMINAL APATHY IN REACHING THE RELIGIOUS LIFE OF THE PEOPLE.

"A distinguished Episcopal bishop, in a speech in New York City sometime since, spoke of the difficulty which the church sometimes experiences in 'getting down from her stilts and walking on the firm ground.' Perhaps the English bishop who best illustrates how this is to be done is, or rather, sad that we should have to say it, *was* Dr. Fraser, of Manchester, who is known to the world at large as a church dignitary. Bishop Fraser's remarks upon secular subjects are always those of a shrewd observer who has a comprehensive mind, and who is never reluctant to take the public into his confidence. He is especially happy in talking to artisans and workingmen.

"In a recent address to workingmen, he told them that tears had been drawn from him by the performance of a 'homely, natural drama,' like 'Black-Eyed Susan.' It is a greater disadvantage to be young, as we suppose the Bishop was, when his tears were drawn at the first sight of a healthy drama, which he tells us he still remembers. And there is a moral in what he said, from his own experience with regard to stage plays, as well as in reference to the pictoral art.

"The plays which the eye looks back upon from a distance—those in which the Bishop discerned 'the best and most natural sentiments' —are those which he thinks the working classes support the most. As with dramas, so with pictures. Within the compass of his brief visits to London, he had found from his visits to the public exhibitions that a 'manly and pure' taste prevailed among the masses of the people. When the church thus comes down to the workingman and honestly tries to enter into his life, the problem of how to reach the masses will solve itself without the help of any tomes of theology.

"The fact of the matter is that the christian church has been criminally apathetic in reaching the moral and religious life of the people. Years ago Mrs. Browning roused the latent pity and sluggish christ-

ianity of the world by her ' Cry of the Children.' Now let the reverend lavender kids and the reverend windbags of the American churches make way for the man of apostolic zeal and christian sympathy,
who shall verify and indeed preach good tidings of joy to all mankind." For the purpose of this argument the quotation may close here.

In addition to the position taken in the foregoing by Bishop Fraser,
the following is a most pointed indorsement of the principal features
of this argument. It is from the discourse delivered by the Rev. Dr.
Lorimer, of Chicago. The topic was: "The Parables of Jesus: The
Dramatic Element in His Ministry."

All these things spake Jesus unto the multitude in parables, and without a parable
spake he not unto them. *Matthew xiii., 34.*

"Pantomime came before language, hieroglyphics before letters,
pictures before books, and the drama before philosophy. Expressive
gestures, poetic imagery, figures of speech, growing into personification, fable and allegory, not only preceded literal discourse and abstract reasoning, but have always surpassed them as vehicles of instruction. When the senses are appealed to, when the imagination is
enlisted, when the emotions are stirred, the impression is more instan-
taneous, vivid and enduring than can be possibly created by means dis-
tinctively recondite and abstruse.

"The drama is narrative in action. It is that form of composition
that represents the personages of the story as living and doing; that re-
veals their thoughts in words and their characters in deeds. It oc-
cupies a prominent position in the literature of all cultivated nations,
and seems to have been originally designed, not exclusively for amusement, but to produce immediate social, religious and political results.
This assumption is abundantly sustained alike by the tragedies of
Æschylus, Sophocles and Euripides, and the comedies of Aristophanes
and Menander. In the first we find repeated political allusions, endea-
vors to restrain advancing radicalism, as in Æschylus, and efforts to
foster freedom, as in Sophocles and in the later pictures of the foibles,
manners, passions of the times, as in Aristophanes.

"It should likewise be borne in mind as confirming the view sug-
gested that the drama, in the earlier stages of its history, was intimate-
ly associated with the great festivals held in honor of the gods that in
Greece, also, it was closely allied to the national religion. The people
of that country celebrated the worship of Dionysius, received from the
Phœnicians, by the performance of comical and tragical plays. This
pleasureable service was paid for out of the public treasury, was gov-

erned by public officials, and was countenanced by the wisest citizens of
the commonwealth—facts which not only lend dignity to these performances, but go to show that they were regarded as eminently practical in their effects. A similar influence is warranted by what is
known by the rise and progress of the drama in England. It first appeared there under the name of ' Mysteries;' then as ' Moralities,' and
afterwards as ' Interludes.'

"The mysteries were exhibitions, more or less replete, of leading
events in the ministry of Christ, the moralities were representations of
an ethical character; while the interludes were decidely humorous and
farcical. These various entertainments were under the patronage of
the church, were given at times in religious houses, and were highly
esteemed by pious and devoted people. Ultimately, however, the
drama divorced itself, or was divorced, from the church, and the modern
theatre came into existence. Since then it has been pretty thoroughly
secularized, and its repeated degradations have given rise to many vexed
questions concerning its influence; but its early alliance with sacred institutions indicates that, in the judgment of antiquity; it was neither
necessarily profane nor pernicious, but was fitted to awaken religious
emotion; kindle holy enthusiasm, and reveal to the poorest understand-
ing the deepest and most gracious of truths.

"The undeniable adaption of dramatic composition to the purest and
noblest interests of humanity explains why it is found to a considerable
extent in the inspired scriptures. That it is there, and there in abun-
dance, all competent critics allow. Of course, their pages will be
searched in vain for anything corresponding to a regular play. But,
while there are no portions of the sacred writing that can be regarded
as dramas in the strict sense of the term, there are several, indeed
many passages which are essentially dramatic in form; narratives, for
instance, where the action, as in the Book of Job, passes before the eye
of the reader, and Revelation, where the events of the personages
connected with them, as in the giving of the decalog, are so vividly
described as to seem perfect realities.

"Our meaning is illustrated by the Homeric poems, where, without
attempting to imitate the play in structure, the plot is unfolded and
carried out by heroes who breathe and move and perform their mighty
deeds as on the mimic stage. The ' Mask of Comus' and the ' Samson Agonistes' of Milton are more perfectly modeled on the pattern of
ancient tragedy than the Epic of Homer, but in many of their characteristics they are not far removed from what we discover in the Old

Testament. They differ in several respects from the tragedies of Shakespeare, and from the ' Faust' of Goethe, and they should rather be classed with dramatic poems than with dramas. From these sources, therefore, may be gathered an adequate idea of what is termed the dramatic element of the Bible.

"A sublime instance of what is meant Moses furnishes in the first chapters of Genesis. How full of startling situations, thrilling movements, absorbing and exciting plots and counterplots, remarkable deliverances and tragical episodes is the career of this Law-giver, and how pathetic and picturesque its close!"

So far we follow Dr. Lorimer. These are the wise and mature utterances of a profound student in the pulpit, and not those of a profane writer for the theatre. Their application is plain. As Hamlet says, "The Play's the thing."

Above all, let the moralist and the church followers remember that the theatre may not only be utilized as a harmless relief and an innocent amusement for the light-hearted, but also as a healing "balm for sore minds"—as "the chief nourisher of life's feast" for man harrassed by incessant struggles, and as a gentle nurse to smoothe the pillow for the woman exhausted by the monotonous drudgery of the household.

Let them not forget that the drama is an effective warning to the wicked, a patient and tireless teacher of both profane and sacred history, and that, next to the church, it is the most fruitful cultivator in man, woman, or child of honor, courage, patriotism, virtue and morality; and last, that its character is always determined by the patronage it receives, and that for all purposes of reform the ultimate power lies with the better element of the masses of the people who patronize it.

MIRACLE-PLAY.   15th CENTURY.

THE ORIGIN OF THE DRAMA.

MIRACLE OR BIBLE PLAYS.

The drama originated amongst the Greeks. It arose from the festivals of Dionysos, a Greek god. "Tragedy" then meant the "goat song," a goat being sacrificed before the hymn was sung. Its proper themes among them were the deeds and sufferings of heroes. With the Greeks it never lost the traces of its religious origin. Æschylus (born 525 B. C.) was the real founder of Greek tragedy. He introduced a second actor, there having been previous to his time but one actor, who carried on the dialogue with the leader of the chorus. The choral song, hitherto the principal feature of the performance, with him became subordinate to the dialogue, and thus the drama was begun. Early in his career the first permanent theatre was erected. He is said to have composed seventy tragedies. Sophocles, who was born thirty years after him, is considered the most perfect writer of ancient drama. He wrote one hundred and thirteen, and Euripides, who was fifteen years younger when he entered on his poetical career, composed ninety-two tragedies. Plato, the great Greek philosopher, (born 429 B. C.) defines tragedy as "an imitation of the noblest life."

The beginnings of dramatic performances amongst the Romans are to be sought in the rural festivities, the occasions of which were private or public religious celebrations. Introduced into the cities, these entertainments received a new impulse from the performances of the Etruscan players, who had been brought into Rome when scenic games, for purposes of religious propitiation, were first held there, about 364 B. C. The regular Roman drama begins about 240 B. C. Cicero, Seneca, and Julius Cæsar himself, wrote plays. The first permanent theatre erected in Rome was 55 B. C. It contained nearly 18,000 seats. The end of the Roman drama was spectacle and show, buffoonery and sensuality, the production of plays being a matter

.of private speculation under contract with the officials charged with the superintendence of amusements. Its final doom, when the faith of the Christian church was acknowledged as the religion of the Roman Empire, was sealed. This doom was not underserved, for the art of acting had begun to pander to the lewd and frivolous. And yet this very church became afterwards, about the 10th century, the nursing mother of the new birth of an art, which seemed incapable of regeneration at that early period.

The origin of dramatic composition in France is not easily fixed. It has been sometimes contended that the traditions of the latin drama were introduced chiefly in the convents by adaptations. There is no doubt that the mystery and the miracle-plays are of a very early date, about the 12th century. In France, they soonest advanced into forms connecting themselves with later growths of the drama.

At Paris, the clerks of the Parliament aquired the right of conducting the popular festivals in 1303, but after the "Confrerie de la Passion," who devoted themselves originally to the performance of passion-plays, had obtained a royal privilege for this purpose in 1402, the former gave themselves up to the production of moralities. The palmy time of both the mysteries and the moralities is in the 15th century.

In Spain, the extant remains of the religious drama date from the 13th or 14th century. Its beginnings presented themselves in an advanced form, and the clergy sought to take the plays entirely under their own control.

The Spanish drama did not for a long period of time seek to emancipate itself from views and forms of religious life. Even in the great age of Spanish dramatic literature it is often most difficult to distinguish between what is to be termed a religious and what a secular play.

In Germany, religious plays were performed as early as the 12th century at the Christmas and Easter festivals. About the 14th century miracle-plays began to be frequently performed. These early German plays have an element of the moralities and were carried on chiefly in carnival time, giving rise to the Shrove-Tuesday plays, called "Fast nachtspiele." The religious drama proper survived in Catholic Germany far beyond the times of the Reformation, and did not disappear in Bavaria and Tyrol till the end of the 18th century. The following on the miracle-plays of England will be found interesting:

I.—The Old Testament.

Miracle Plays which are usually called the source and the foundation of the drama of England, consisted altogether of Scripture characters and differed from the "Moral Plays" which were represented by allegorical characters. The Miracle Plays deviated afterwards almost imperceptibly into the latter by the gradual intermixture of allegory with sacred history, until the former were finally entirely superseded by the latter, which in turn gave way to tragedy and comedy.

At the outset it was customary to perform these bible-dramas in and about churches on scaffolds erected for the purpose, and to borrow horses, harness, and other paraphnalia, even hallowed vestments from the monasteries for their elaborate production. Besides the performances at the places hereafter spoken of, such exhibitions took place at York, Newcastle-upon-Tyne, Durham, Lancaster, Leeds, Preston, Kendall, Bristol, Witney, Cambridge, Manningtree and other places; about the middle of the thirteenth century.

George Nazianzen is known as the inventor of them in France in the fourth century, but the first Miracle-Play ever introduced into England from France was brought out at Dunstable in 1119, and was performed by the scholars of one Geoffrey, who was a member of the University of Paris before his attainment to the highest dignity in the Monastry at St. Albans. Those subsequently known as the Widkirk Miracle-Plays, as appears from MSS. in the British Museum, were without any introductory matter, while those of Chester were preceded by a proclamation which was made by standard bearers in various parts of the city on St. George's day before the performance commenced. They all began on Whit-Monday and continued until Wednesday. Up to the reign of Edward III. in 1338, they were performed with few exceptions in the French language, the exception being those performed in Latin.

But after that time they were, through the efforts of Ralph Higdon, performed in the English tongue. Higdon had to make no less than three trips to Rome before he was permitted to translate the French and Latin plays into English and receive permission for their regular production in that language.

The first of the Widkirk plays was entitled "The Creation," and included the rebellion and the expulsion of Lucifer. After the work of the creation the Deity, so ran the story, descended from his throne and went out, when Lucifer usurps it. The plot then closely followed in its main features the incidents as related in the Old Testament.

The first two Chester plays treated the same period and incidents of Scripture History, as did also the first two of the Coventry plays. The third Widkirk play was "Noah's Flood," which was got up in a most elaborate manner, especially the Ark. The fourth play was "Abraham and Isaac." The fifth, sixth and seventh concluded that portion which was included in the Old Testament. The last of these was a very remarkable play relating to the departure of the Israelites from Egypt. In the course of the play the seven plagues were represented falling on the Egyptians. After a long conference of the Deity with Moses, the latter wrought the miracles before Pharaoh, commencing with the conversion of his rod into a serpent and ending with the death of the first born of all the Egyptians; after which Pharaoh having yielded an unwilling consent, Moses and his people take their departure. Pharaoh and his host pursuing them, were supposed to be suddenly drowned, the last words of the King being

"Now Mon we pay for all our dede,"—

when Moses concluded the play by a long speech to his people.

In the Chester series the fifth play is the last which relates to the Old Testament, while in the Coventry plays it closes with the sixth play.

II.—THE NEW TESTAMENT.

In looking over the Widkirk series we find that the "New Testament Plays" open with "The Salutation, Conception and Birth of Christ," introducing Augustus Cæsar, the Deity, Gabriel, the Virgin Mary, Joseph and Elizabeth. Whilst in the Chester series Cæsar is called Octavianus. The Coventry plays from the 8th to the 15th are entirely taken up with matters relating to the birth of Christ not contained in any other series. An allegorical character named *Contemplation* is prominent in the earlier of these latter plays who acts as a Prologue-Speaker, and who explains and moralizes on the events represented.

In the eleventh of these pageants the progress of the incidents is interrupted by what is called *the Parliament of Heaven*, in which, among several, the Father and the Son are speakers, and Gabriel descends and explains to Joseph the secret of the conception and future birth of the Saviour. In the 14th play two new Allegorical parts are introduced called *First* and *Second Detractor*.

In the 15th Coventry Play occurs an incident such as is still found in the Christmas Carols. The Virgin Mary on seeing a cherry tree longs for some of the fruit, when Joseph tells her that he who is the father of her child can procure it for her, and thereupon the tree instantly bows down to her hand.

In the Widkirk Manuscripts are found two plays on "The Adoration of the Shepherds," in which *First*, *Second* and *Third Pastor* are prominent characters. These productions were given about 1377. The Shepherds in the "Coventry Plays" are extremely learned in the prophecies. Herod is first introduced in the 13th of the Widkirk plays. He is astonished that there are other kings besides himself, when told of the coming of Melchior, Belshazzar and Jaspar, the kings of Tarsus, Taba and Araby; he being very boastful of his power "in one scene" breaks the sword he wears, in sheer rage. The kings enter riding real horses, and an Angel warns them not to return through the dominions of Herod. The chief action of the 15th Widkirk pageant is the slaughter of the Innocents.

In the Chester play on this subject Herod's own son is killed by a mistake; Herod is taken suddenly ill, then dies, and the devil appears and carries him off and the play closes with the return of Mary and Joseph to the scene.

In the Coventry plays on the other hand, Herod sits down to a banquet with his Knights when a personification of Death appears "nakyd and of poor aray," who states that he is "God's Messenger" and he slays Herod. In Widkirk and Chester this play included the dispute of Christ and the Doctors in the temple which constitutes a separate play in the Coventry series.

We have now about reached the year 1507. The succeeding plays had for their subjects "Christ's Baptism and Temptation," "The Woman taken in adultery," "The Treachery of Judas" and "The Crucifixion." The 32nd of the Coventry Plays was the most realistic upon the latter subject.

The 22nd of the Widkirk series is "The casting of the Dice." "The Descent of Christ into Hell" was one of every known collection of Miracle-plays and was very popular on account of its scope for display. In it Jesus finally frees Adam, Eve and the prophets.

The play of "The Resurrection" is treated very much in the same style in the three sets of the plays following closely the account in the New Testament. The 25th and 26th of the Widkirk plays treat of the appearance of Christ to Cleophas, Luke and the rest of the Apostles; the same subject is treated of in the 18th and 19th of the Chester plays.

The 27th at Widkirk relates to the Ascension. The 23rd at Chester was called "The Antichrist;" in it Christ assumes almighty power, raises two men from the dead, dies himself and comes to life again.—Enoch and Elias appear to disprove his claim to be the Messiah. Antichrist in his fury slays Enoch and Elias along with many others. The Archangel Michael for this slays Antichrist, when demons appear and carry off his body, whereupon Enoch and Elias arise and ascend with the Angel Michael to heaven. None of the other series embraced this subject.

The opening of the 28th play "The Last Judgment" is wanting among the MSS. of Widkirk, but in the finale the Saviour, after a long speech in which he shows his wounds, dismisses four good souls to heaven and four bad ones to hell; in the finale of the "Judgement" at Chester, the demons appear and drag the wicked away "ever to live in woe," while four Evangelists conclude the whole of this series of plays by impressing upon the audience the truth of their gospels.

At Coventry the 42nd play was called "Doomsday," and was produced about 1577. The MSS. of these plays of which J. Payne Collier gives full details in his "Annals of the English Stage" are covered with marginal notes containing the stage directions, showing that they were always produced under church supervision, with great regard to completeness and detail, in some instances evidencing the use of four separate stages, one of which had contrivances for infernal regions with "helle ondyr neth that stage."

The accounts of Miracle-plays in London are comparatively few, but many were performed and frequently repeated, especially during the reign of Queen Mary, and as they were calculated to extend and enforce the tenets of the then dominant religion, they were encouraged by the Public Authorities.

In 1556 a regular stage-play of the passions of Christ was presented at Grey-Friars in London on Corpus-Christi-Day before the Lord Mayor, the Privy Council and many great estates of the realm.

In 1557 it was repeated at the same theatre, and was again produced on St. Olave's day of that year, as a stage-play in St. Olave's Church in Silver Street with the following theatre company in the cast: Richard and John Birche, Richard Cooke, R. Skinner, Thomas Southey and John Browne. This was at a time when severe measures were thought necessary against theatrical representations which tended to obstruct the progress of reformation.

Collier shows clearly that Miracle-plays were constantly acted at Chester until 1577; at Coventry until 1591; at York until late in the 16th Century; at New Castle until 1598, and at Lancaster, Preston and Kendall until the beginning of the reign of James I. After 1603 the "Moral-plays" had been slowly encroaching and superceding them by degress. The last known writer of any of the Miracle-plays was one John Bale, parish priest of Thorndon, Suffolk, his last works being "God's Promises," "Christ's Temptation," " John the Baptist" and the "Three Laws of Nature," the MSS. of which are to be found in a most complete state of preservation in the British Museum in London.

MOSES AND PHARAOH.

A NEW DEPARTURE IN STAGE LITERATURE.

BY PROF. JOHN FRASER.

GRAND OPERA HOUSE, CHICAGO.   *January 15th, 1883.*

FRIEND FRASER :—I have appointed to-morrow evening, say, at 8 o'clock, to hear the Biblical play, "Moses & Pharaoh," read :

♦ Will you be here at that time. I want your judgment on it.

Your friend,   JOHN A. HAMLIN.

(Note in pencil by Prof. Fraser.) Jan'y 17th. Heard play read by author, Mr. ——, in presence of Mr. Jno. Allen and Mr. Hamlin. Good, strong, play.

The above letter from Manager John A. Hamlin not only shows the estimation in which the judgment of the late Prof. Fraser upon dramatic matters, was held amongst those most interested, but will also account for the elaborate criticism upon the play referred to, which the publishers found along with above letter amongst the numerous MS. of this sharp and caustic writer, who, for some time acted as dramatic critic for the *Tribune*, and whose connection with the stage on both sides of the Atlantic gained for him the esteem and friendship of all the leading actors and actresses of the day, many of whom such as Irving, Modjeska, Salvini, Rhea, Booth, &c., &c., have repeatedly thanked him for the honesty of his criticism, although admitting that they smarted considerably under his lash. (The Publishers.)

To lovers of Drama and Art in the high and old acceptation of these words, so far at least as concerns drama,—are becoming as obsolete as the accepted meaning of Tennyson's Gentleman."

> "Defamed by every Charlatan,
> "And put to all ignoble use,
> "The grand old name of Gentleman."

To lovers of the pure and the true in Drama, I say the American Stage of to-day presents a ghastly sight.

In one corner we have "We, Us & Co." being tossed "Over the Garden Wall" by a "Tin Soldier" who happens not to be "In the Swim" but "In Hot Water," and in another an acrobatic monstrosity which it would be profanity to call even a "farce" and the only re-

THEATRE AT BATH. ERECTED PRIOR TO 1800.

deeming feature in which is the performances of some dogs and a donkey—and all these exhibitions of idiocy and horse play patronized by thousands, while Lawrence Barrett's "Francesca Da Remini" and anybody's "Shakespeare" barely pays expenses.

In view of all this we felt inclined to cry with Hamlet, "The world is out of joint," and still again, "Oh cursed spite," would that the man were born to set it right! That, we say was what the writer felt moved to cry until he went early this week to hear read a new play on a subject certainly new to the theatre of to-day. From having heard the play in question one is constrained to believe not only that its author is the much wanted dramatist and his play the much wanted play required to inaugurate a new and noble departure in drama, but that general readers will be interested in a brief synopsis of the drama itself.

To begin with the subject is Biblical and the hero Moses. Let not any one be shocked by this. Even those who shudder at the idea of a "Passion Play," portraying the earthly career and sufferings of our Saviour, need have no feeling of aversion to a reverent and serious dramatic treatment of the life of the great Hebrew law maker.

As a fact and apart altogether from its divine origin, this is one of the secrets of the extraordinary interest and popularity of the Bible— no book in existence is so uniformly and intensely dramatic as this Book of books.

Why only think of Jacob, Daniel, David, Saul, St. Paul and St. John, not to mention a score of others—what splendid—what inexaustible material do not these names suggest to the creative writer, be he novelist, dramatist or poet, for effective treatment.

Nor is there any reason in the world why their careers—for after all they were merely human, and as such are within the scope of criticism and reverent poetical treatment—should not be made the subject of Drama, which, indeed—at least in its early history in Europe—was based almost entirely on the Bible, the favorite heroes being Adam, Noah and Christ. But to return to the drama more immediately under notice—and with all reverence be it said—from the Christ, there is no character in the entire range of the Bible whose career offers so many splendid points for superb dramatic treatment as Moses.

In the play read to us the other evening, entitled, "Moses & Pharaoh," Moses is the grand central figure, round whom the tremendous events of the great drama surge and circle, and in whom the interest centres. From first to last the play is one of intense interest—so intense as at times to be almost painful. Event crowds on event, one tragic incident succeeds another, and all combine to sweep the listener along with such irresistible and ever increasing force to the triumphant close that the interest is never allowed to flag for a single moment, but is hurried on breathless and unresisting to the final overthrow of the Pharaoh and the triumph of Moses and his people.

And here it may be as well to quote the author's own idea of his work as given in his brief preface. He says: "This play is an effort at dramatic treatment of a biblical subject to illustrate seriously its historical grandeur. Of all the ancient personages of whom the Bible gives us a clearly drawn picture, Moses, with one exception, is by far the greatest character. None compare with him in philosophy, in grandeur of thought, of action and of aim.

"The afflictions of the Hebrew race under the tyranny of Egypt's Kings and the sacred mysteries of the inner temple of Isis, the goddess revered by the Egyptians as the great benefactress of their country, are the surroundings in which the character of Moses was formed and where it grew to its perfection. As one of the royal household (by reason of his adoption by the King's daughter) he was educated by the 'King's priests,' and was no doubt intended for the highest duties among them."

The Drama consists of a Prologue and five acts. The prologue is extremely dramatic. The entrance into the house of Amram (the father of Moses) of Pharaoh's emissaries in search of the son Moses in order to destroy him in accordance with Pharaoh's horrible decree that all male children should be murdered, the flight, through a side-door at the same time, of Jochobeth the mother and Miriam the sister of the infant Moses, to hide the child in its fragile cradle amid the bulrushes of the Nile, the finding of Moses by Thermutis the Royal Princess and the discomfiture by her of Pharaoh's soldiers hot in pursuit of the babe, all go to make up an act of intense and cumulative interest for the prologue.

Then follow in the succeeding acts forty years later—the meeting of Moses and Joshua in the land of Goshen, the return to Egypt of Moses to liberate his people, the discomfiture of the haughty Pharaoh Sesostris, and his final overthrow in the Red Sea.

It is almost impossible to imagine a more dramatic story, or one more abounding in incidents of which the scenic artist could make more effective use. Think of the triumphal return of Sesostris and his entry in state into his capital at the head of his victorious army flushed with victory, and then imagine the alternations of passion displayed by the same proud king as he finds his High Priests put to shame by Moses, nor loses faith in his own high destiny until he sees his wife and only son and heir fall victims to the plague!

And following hard upon all this the attempted passage through the Red Sea; the collapse of the mighty walls of water, the complete ruin of the great Egyptian army and the triumph of the Israelites with Moses at their head to the discomfiture of Korah and the other conspirators against their great leader.

This hasty synopsis of the play, imperfect as it is, may suggest its dramatic interest and effect. In keeping with its high character is the noble simplicity of the language.

There is here no illegitimate striving after effect; everything is stated in the simplest and most consistent way possible; not a word from first to last and not a scene or incident suggests in the remotest degree irreverence. The characters are all strongly drawn and stand out boldly from the canvas besides being nicely contrasted, with the result that their several characteristics are prominently shown.

It seems indeed exactly the sort of drama that is needed at present to attract a new class of theatregoers and again recover those who have been estranged from the stage, as this play provides in one dramatic unity the many different kinds of attractions—only raised by the greatness of the theme to a higher altitude—which are now popular. It would be a worthy acquisition to stage literature and unquestionably a boon to thousands, now ignorant on the subject, to learn by the means of this drama of the throes and trials through which the Hebrew race passed in ancient times.

Do you want Spectacle? here you have it—finer if need be than ever the Kiralfi Brothers dreamed of. Development of character? Moses, whom Professor Max Mueller places at the head of the list of all the great religious leaders, is a life study by himself. Human conflict? What conflict more intense than that of the oppressed Jews with the Egyptian barbarians, the struggles of the slaves against their inhuman masters, the appeals of Moses, the wisest of his time, to ignorant brutality. Sensationalism and opportunities for the exhibition of the ingenuity of stage mechanism? What better chances than the burning bush near Mount Horeb, the pyramids, the city of Memphis, the grand entrance of Pharaoh, the marvelous expositions of the miracles performed by Moses in the sight of the people.

Take the overthrow of the Pharaoh Sesostris, the discomfiture of

the priests—could anything be more startling than the final destruction
of the Egyptian's army in the Red Sea.

Lastly there is this to say and, after all, this (like a lady's postscript)
contains the gist of the matter—the author has produced a drama that
if properly presented seems to us admirably calculated to meet a new
demand on the part of the public, to supply a new want and to foster
new tastes.

To begin with, the play of "Moses and Pharaoh" appeals to the
lovers of ancient history as well as to the admirers of the sensational,
giving almost unlimited opportunity for splendor of scenic display; in
the next place, it provides that rapid development of an intensely interesting plot ending in a thrilling dramatic climax, which is the great
object of all eminent dramatists as it is the chief delight of all intelligent theatre-goers. What more likely to claim our attention than
the illustration of the sufferings of a down trodden race, inflicted at
the hands of cruel masters, inflicted upon the unfortunate by the powerful—human sufferings and wrongs heaped upon the heads of the
weak by the strong thousands of years ago. These appeal to our
sympathy as deeply to-day as though endured and committed but yesterday.

And, which is perhaps more immediately to our purpose "Moses"
appeals to that large class of moral church going and pulpit filling
citizens, who have been educated to believe little good of the stage and
its productions.

The production of this play will encourage the march of education
in a groove that has been lost sight of. It will foster the cause of
religion in a liberal channel as it is bound to arouse a new interest in
biblical history through the noblest of human amusements. It will
attract alike the attention of the student of history or religion and the
ordinary patron of stage plays. The presentation of our Saviour on
a stage might well shock thousands of intelligent people,—though on
the "Oberamergan" stage it deeply impressed everybody—and this arises
simply from the reverence and awe with which the Christ is generally
regarded. But with regard to Moses no such feeling ought to prevail.
Moses never pretended to be of divine origin in the sense that the
Christ did. He was simply a man such as most of us are, only, of
course, a great deal wiser and nobler. To represent him therefore is
no sacrilege, and ought not, so long as the representation is reverent,
shock the nicest sensibilities. A prominent divine only the other day
said, "We live in a day of reforms. Thus is the spirit in the air that

"is constantly organizing movements that look toward the systematic "assailing of evil and the cure of sin."

We agree perfectly with the gentleman. If the worthy speaker means to show his earnestness in behalf of effective movements of this character he and others of his cloth should encourage, nay, urge the utilization of the most powerful factor for the purpose of familiarizing that great mass of his fellow beings, who will never come within the reach of his own limited voice—but who do patronize the theatre—with the life of the first and most prominent reformers of the Old Testament.

More than this, the dramatist attempts to do in his own way what George Ebers, by his admirable Egyptian novels has tried to do in his. He revives a long buried age and by the aid of the story, scenery and drama tries, and we should say successfully, to give this age of ours a vivid and realistic idea of those countries, customs, peoples and events with which the Bible has made all Christian communities vaguely acquainted.

In this way the new drama of "Moses and Pharaoh" seems to us to fully meet the requirements of a public taste that has been evolved out of an inevitable revulsion against the wretched sort of drama in vogue of late and an equally inevitable desire, conscious or unconscious, for better things. Believing that "Moses and Pharaoh" will meet this taste—will nobly inaugurate a great and much needed reform,—the writer wishes it and its author a healthy "God-speed."

ART OR AMUSEMENT?

The storm heeds not our protest or our blame,
    When it obeys no laws:
The ocean feels no pang or grief or shame
    When wrecking what it draws.
The vulgar love the vicious and the low—
    The demon rules within;
The roaring sea and reckless storm but show
    That passion's rule breeds sin.

Is the profession of the actor an art, or is it mere stage-craft, serviceable only as amusement for the thoughtless multitude? This is a serious question bearing on the future of the theatre. By a majority of people, among whom, it is to be regretted, are many of the disciples of the stage and the drama, it is looked upon and treated as a means of amusement only, and not as an art. This is a sad mistake, which, if it were universally accepted and acted on as correct, would eventually work the utter debasement of the theatre.

A majority of the human race, measured by generations, is undeniably but little removed from primeval savagery in judgment, in taste, in inclination and in desire, when left to follow its own natural instincts. Civilization has not succeeded and never will succeed in entirely weeding out of this continuous majority the inherent brutal instincts of barbarism. This majority would prefer to witness for its amusement bull and prize-fights, gladiatorial shows, the vulgar antics of the buffoon, and the exhibitions of open licentiousness, were they only permitted by the police to do so.

The advanced civilization of the minority, of course, frowns on such shows, but the dormant common sentiment of the majority would patronize and enjoy them, if public opinion and the authorities did not cow them down and restrain them. This is the same majority which gloats over recitals of brutality or stories of salacious fiction, and which prefers to look upon the illustrations of vulgar monstrosities or lewd-

44

THEATRE AT WINDSOR. ERECTED 1793.

ness rather than peruse the works of literary masters or dwell on mas-
terpieces of pictorial or sculptural art. Ignorant bullies, who can
"knock the stuffing" out of some rival "bruiser," can draw more money
by their exhibitions than can the most renowned scholar. The former
will have a larger following to the grave than will the philanthropist
or the statesman.

The mercenary theatrical speculators, without respect or judgement—the superficial critics lacking both training as well as enthusiasm for their calling—and the "playmakers," without the souls of
poets, or even dramatic instinct—these are crowding the art of the actor
from its place, by insisting that the theatre is nothing but a caterer to
the amusement of those who will pay the largest returns. These
greedy cormorants, together with the thoughtless patrons of the theatre, have for years past been digging the grave of dramatic art.

The brutal exhibitions of the ancients were not as demoralizing
in their time, or as debasing to public taste, as are many of the present
"shows" on the stage, or as are the pictorial nudities disgracing the
dead walls and the shop windows.

The following is from a late number of one of the most pretenti-
ous of the exclusively "theatrical papers" of New York. Read it, and
stand abashed at its closing sentence. It says: "It is in the female
department of the cast that Mr. C.'s system works most banefully
This stage manager seems to have made up his mind that it matters
not how his women sing, so long as they show enough of their well-
proportioned persons to please the male portion of the audience, for he
has dressed his chorus in costumes that would almost make a hardened
sinner blush, if for nothing else than sympathy for the women, who
were compelled, by the hard exigencies of the situation, to wear them.
They came as near absolute nakedness as anything that has ever been
so far attempted in New York. *But let it pass, for it may accomplish its evident intention of drawing money to the house.*"

And this performance takes place in one of the handsomest theatres
in New York, frequented by the young elite of the city, a house in
which the late mayor and the millionaires of the town are stock-
holders.

What will be next in order for this mercenary speculator and his
confreres, whose sole argument no doubt is that he must furnish what
the public want and will pay for, when he can no longer make money
with the present "article?"

Once upon a time—not so very long ago, but before the days of

Alfieri, Porta and Goldoni in Italy, of Lope de Vega and Calderon in Spain, of Corneille, Racine and Moliere in France,—before the days of Kyd, Marlowe and Shakespeare in England, and of Hans Sachs, of Weise, of Klay, of Velthen, of Gottsched and of Lessing in Germany —before the days of these pioneers in dramatic literature, the stage was in the possession of vulgar clowns, and had sunk to a mere "place of amusement." It had lost its artistic hold. But then came these Titans of dramatic poetry, interpreted by mighty exponents on the stage, and they rescued the institution and raised it to its proper place among the arts throughout the civilized world. True, none of these great men of the past possessed much wealth,—some of them died in poverty,—but they gloried in their work, and they live forever in the temple of fame.

To-day, however, the theatrical speculator, controling the shallow critics, the mercenary columns of the press, and the mechanical "playmaker," all assisted by the shameless women and the clowns and buffons of the stage, are working hand in hand to drag dramatic art down lower and lower, and are thus daily corrupting public taste.

Dramatic art is out in the open sea with unprincipled desperadoes at the helm. In their blind avarice they do not see the danger which threatens their craft. Will it reach the shore? It took a century to raise it from its depths of old. It required the genius of dramatic giants to accomplish it. It took the life long labors of many of them to fix it firmly in its high place. Sustain it as an art, for as a mere source of amusement its glorious days are numbered. The equals of the great saviours of the past are possibly not yet born. Only a few short years more of the same efforts at its debasement and the better element of its patrons may be entirely estranged from it.

The unscrupulous speculator must be banished, the vulgar clown must retire, and the brazen exhibitress of her secret charms must be expelled. The well-meaning manager, the thoughtful actor, the conscientious critic and the serious dramatist, must combine to interest the better element now largely estranged from the temple. Serious efforts must be made, sacrifices must not be feared, and a new constituency must be found who will support true merit. The crowd in and out of the theatre must be brought to its senses.

> He who lacks command for the drama's restoration
> Should wield a trowel or square a stone to aid its elevation:
> He who lacks for this the chance or skill of hand
> Should mix the mortar, slack the lime or wheel the sand.

THEATRICAL EXTRAVAGANCE.

Uncalled for extravagance in connection with the theatre deserves to be rebuked most emphatically and promptly, the same as it does in connection with everything else in real life, because such extravagance is a positive injury to dramatic art. What can justify a manager in expending $7,000 or $8,000 on stage furniture, to be used in one short scene only in an untried play, the staying powers of which he is positively incapable of foreseeing? Even if he were, what right has he to expect (which he surely must) the public to pay, by high prices of admission, for a few moments' glance, during a short run, at such uncalled for extravagance? It is clearly inartistic extravagence, and an imposition on the stage as an institution, as such expenditure alone could not give life to a poor play, if such it should prove to be.

It is an inartistic waste of money, for realism carried to that extent on the stage is inartistic, while it may be well enough in the field of art furniture for the special indulgence of the millionaire. *Artistic imitation* of the real article is what belongs to the stage, and it is that which we desire to admire there and not the real article itself—not even *real* tears, if they are brought forth through physical ailments in those who shed them. Art ends where reality begins. Nothing real but *real* actors and actresses, with artistic natures, is what we want on the stage. As for everything else behind the curtain, the better the imitation the greater the artistic achievement.

This brings me to another extravagance in connection with the stage. I mean the extravagant *expectations* of certain actors and managers which they attach to what they consider the only evidence of merit and success of plays now-a-days. What right have they to consider such a play only worthy of cultivation and production, which by a long unbroken run during years will bring them all fortunes?

What right has either one of them to look upon all other plays as unworthy of his attention? The repertory of the stage can not be too large. A manufacturer may sometimes hope to make a fortune out of the manufacturing of one special class of goods, but certainly never out of the first lot he manufactures without ever improving upon his wares, if improvement is possible. Most of the latter-day critics have fallen into the same error, and they will hasten to condemn a new work on its first production unless they can foresee years of uninterrupted performances in it. It is the extravagance first alluded to, together with the latter, which keeps many a deserving drama buried and unheard of, and many able pens away from dramatic work.

Besides this, the latter-day extravagant realism in the productions of the works of temporarily successful playmakers is a great injury to the stage and its literature. They insist that that is what the public wants. Strictly construed, it is not a question what the public wants. The public is a great big baby—the baby is sometimes pleased with a rattle, sometimes tickled with a straw, and generally delighted when permitted to smash everything within reach at the table. It is dangerous to give the baby what it wants.

Sound moral problems should always underlie stage plays, whether comic or serious. There can be no life to a play without them. This is too frequently ignored altogether, while the past has taught that therein consists the only merit which gives lasting qualities to a play. The naked realism of a Zola and his weak English and American imitators, simply revealing the slums of our matter-of-fact age without instruction and redeeming sunshine can only be shortlived.

Interesting plots within the limits of probability, logically constructed, each succeeding scene the natural outgrowth of a preceding one, with characters consistently drawn into action in harmony with the story or the subject under treatment, the whole written in terse language with effective finale to each act culminating for comedy in a happy, and for tragic material in a serious denouement, such plays should always meet with respectful considerations from managers, actors and critics, for by such productions they will surely interest a half-way intelligent audience. The fair treatment of such work by managers and by the public will encourage dramatic authorship among men of literary ability.

The phrase of "going to the theatre to be amused" is a very careless one—in fact, it is mostly erroneously indulged in. Persons using it really mean that they want a performance to *interest* them. When it does this, whether it is of a serious or of a comic character, it gives them pleasure, it charms them. That is what they want. A good story graphically depicted and artistically illustrated by intelligent actors, in appropriate habiliments with good stage settings and scenery—such performances properly varied from time to time at endurable seasons of the year, and at reasonable rates of admission will attract a living share of public support. If such plays have literary merit besides, they are sure to live long. Those plays which have outlived a generation or more, were excellent from a dramatic as well as from a literary standpoint. Any such written to-day will not require an $8,000 set of stage furniture for a reasonably successful production, as was recently thought necessary in one of our Chicago theatres for the play entitled "A Moral Crime."

DRAMATIC CRITICISM.

It is not particularly creditable to simply find fault with apparent abuses around us or with the special work of individuals or of a class, unless the fault-finder can suggest some remedy for the correction of the former or point out more honorable methods or a better line of action for the latter.

It is not intended herewith to assail any class of literary or journalistic workers, but it will be readily conceded to be a fact that there is much cause for complaint against the common run of recent stage work and against the lack of literary merit of the dramatic productions on the English-speaking stage of late years. While this is undeniable, there is also much cause for fault-finding with the average ability of the dramatic critic of the daily press and with the frequent worthlessness, if not dangerous tendency, of its criticism. It may not be going too far to insist that the latter fact is much the cause of the former state of things.

An able writer in the *North American Review* on the "Decline of the Drama," as long ago as 1877, insisted that its low condition was largely attributable "to the mischievous influence of the newspaper press." This fault, however, is more the result of the careless system of assignments of this class of journalistic work than otherwise.

There are honorable exceptions to every rule, but there are only a few dramatic critics, specially qualified for this work by study and experience, now engaged upon the daily press of this country. As a class, they do not understand themselves so clearly as behooves the high and responsible vocation which they are filling. Ability and fitness are not the rule among the writers who are entrusted with the passing of judgment upon the work for and on the English-speaking stage.

Mrs. Kendal, one of the principal actresses of the London theatres, in a recent lecture on the drama, before the Social Science Congress of Birmingham, among other things said: "I do not think the press

THEATRE AT PORTSMOUTH. ERECTED 1761.

of the present day does all that it might do for the welfare of the drama. Criticism, if it is to be worth anything, should surely be *criticism*, but nowadays the writing of a picturesque article, replete with eulogy or the reverse, seems to be the him of the theatrical reviewer."

The able editor of an English dramatic monthly, who is also the critic of a London daily paper, in speaking of the degeneracy of theatrical criticism and the utter indifference of audiences to the dignity of dramatic art, says: "Who then, is to blame for the falling off in respect and reverence of such as are presumably interested in the theatre, and how are we to account for the want of high tone and dignity in audiences except on very special occasions, and at theatres that command our utmost courtesy? I do not hesitate to say that we, journalists and writers, are most of all to blame. Since the era of smart-writing and personal talk about plays, the character of audiences has visibly deteriorated.

"Nowadays, writers fill their columns with base and scurrilous chatter, cruel and cowardly insinuations are printed of ladies on the stage, private conversations are peached upon by well-dressed spies and published for the edification of a curious public; the theatre swarms with the agents of scandal-mongering chroniclers, and these *journalists*, these hangers on and toadies, are made welcome in every theatre, nay invited with groveling deference; the inner life of actors and actresses is exposed under a magnifying glass; authors are put up in a pillory and pelted with misrepresentations by scribes who are a disgrace to their calling. For this disease there is no cure; the age permits it, and we pass on from bad to worse. Surfeit alone may bring relief."

These are the words of an honorable exception to the common run of his craft. The dramatic critic's duty and his position properly defined make him the protector of the drama, the teacher of the actor, and the guide in dramatic taste of the patrons of the theatre. He should be a deep reader of human nature and its characteristics, be thoroughly acquainted with the principles and craft of dramatic composition and the art of acting, an enthusiastic student of dramatic literature and its exponents, and, not the least, *an experienced spectator of performances.*

What an irreparable injury to the taste and character of a generation of theatre-goers and newspaper readers it is, to find young people engaged in this noble vocation, who are often incapable of appreciating deserving work and whose allotted space is filled by elaborating upon mediocrity and vulgarity, who not only lack a proper knowledge

of human nature, which it takes years to acquire, but who are even
wanting in training and experience, in inclination and taste, and, worst
of all, who have no enthusiasm for the matters appertaining to the
stage, for the high aims of its honorable followers, or for the meritor-
ious productions and achievements of the past and present! They are
not infrequently mercenary in character or full of malice, and not so
constituted by nature that they could give a fair and unprejudiced
opinion on any subject or on the earnest work of any man, no matter
how lofty his aim.

In New York City it was even found several years ago that a
number of theatrical critics of the daily press were actually upon the
regular payrolls of several of the most prominent theatres.

The *theatrical reporter* might have his distinct place on the staff
to make up interesting paragraphs of gossip. He may gather his material from behind the scenes, from the clubs and the public resorts of
the professional people. All of these places, the serious critic should
avoid professionally. His professional attention should be directed to
plays and players on the stage only.

The news-gatherer may fawn upon those who furnish him with
"pointers." The critical judge should be perfectly independent. He
should have strong likes and dislikes, but he should shun those on
whom he passes sentence, and his opinions should appear in the dignified
columns of the editorial page, the same as is the rule in all other matters of importance, and the work should be entrusted to able and
honest pens.

What do we find, however, to be the actual condition of things?
The same "critic" who is thought competent to expatiate upon the
pleasures of the skating rink and the monstrosities of the dime museum, or the attractions of the circus or prize ring, wields the rod
under the general head-line of "Amusements," over the heads of a
Salvini, a Booth, a Barrett, a Ristori, a Janauschek, and over Sardou
as well as Shakespeare. In no other branch of American journalism
is this indifference so lamentably the rule as in this most important one
of dramatic criticism, which necessitates so high a degree of ability and
enthusiasm to make the better best.

The critic who is not ardent himself can have no sympathy with
those who are ardent, and ardor is an indispensible requisite to art-
taste and to the comprehension of artistic merit. Nothing great in art
can be accomplished or appreciated without enthusiasm. It develops
what is high, noble and true, and it encourages the serious and lofty
aims of life.

Enthusiasm will not be dictated to by fashion, or say sharp things of a personal nature, or mock at sentiment, or lend itself to languid indifference or vulgar wit any more than it will to the indorsement of vicious or dangerous stage or dramatic work; but ability and experience, backed by enthusiasm in the critic, will ever lay aside *personal* likes and dislikes, applaud genuine sentiment and merit, recognize ability and commend true genius in others, and thus assist dramatic and stage art to hold its own and wield its proper and undeniably great influence upon the taste and character of an intelligent and liberal people. Let the newspaper press raise the standard of its dramatic criticism by all means.

THE PRESENT DEGRADATION OF THE THEATRE.

LAMENTATIONS FROM THE RANKS—BREAKING THE SPELL.

One of the most cultivated men engaged in theatrical management at present in New York City—whose past has been an honor to the stage and to the profession, although not himself an actor—a man of intelligence and thought and a director of experience of the best class of stock-theatres—an earnest advocate of elevating dramatic doctrines —a man whose opinions in connection with any thing affecting plays, actors and theatres are entitled to respect—this man is reported to have lately said, "I think that the stage to day is a greater evil than any other institution we have. Nothing does so much harm to the young "men and young women of this city. The stage is now in one of "those critical conditions that it passes through about once in every "generation. Only this one seems to be unusually severe and hard to "get over." Of course he qualifies his broad assertions by applying them only to the theatres where the present-day low absurdities and nude burlesques are the rule.

In 1883 one of the oldest and most respected of New York actors, now dead, said, "I believe the present condition of the drama, both "from a moral and artistic point of view, to be a subject for regret." In conclusion, however, he stated that he could "call to mind no play, "old or new, where either the *worthy* preacher of religion or the *de-* "*vout* believer in its promises is treated with contempt."

An actress, who is a woman of remarkable intelligence and wide experience on the stage in this and foreign countries, says upon this subject: "The present condition of the dramatic art in America is not a matter for congratulation. The combination system has pretty nearly destroyed theatric work as an exponent of distinctive art. The remedy? Ah, that is plain enough; the stock companies must be revived. They are the schools of acting in which the dramatic talent is

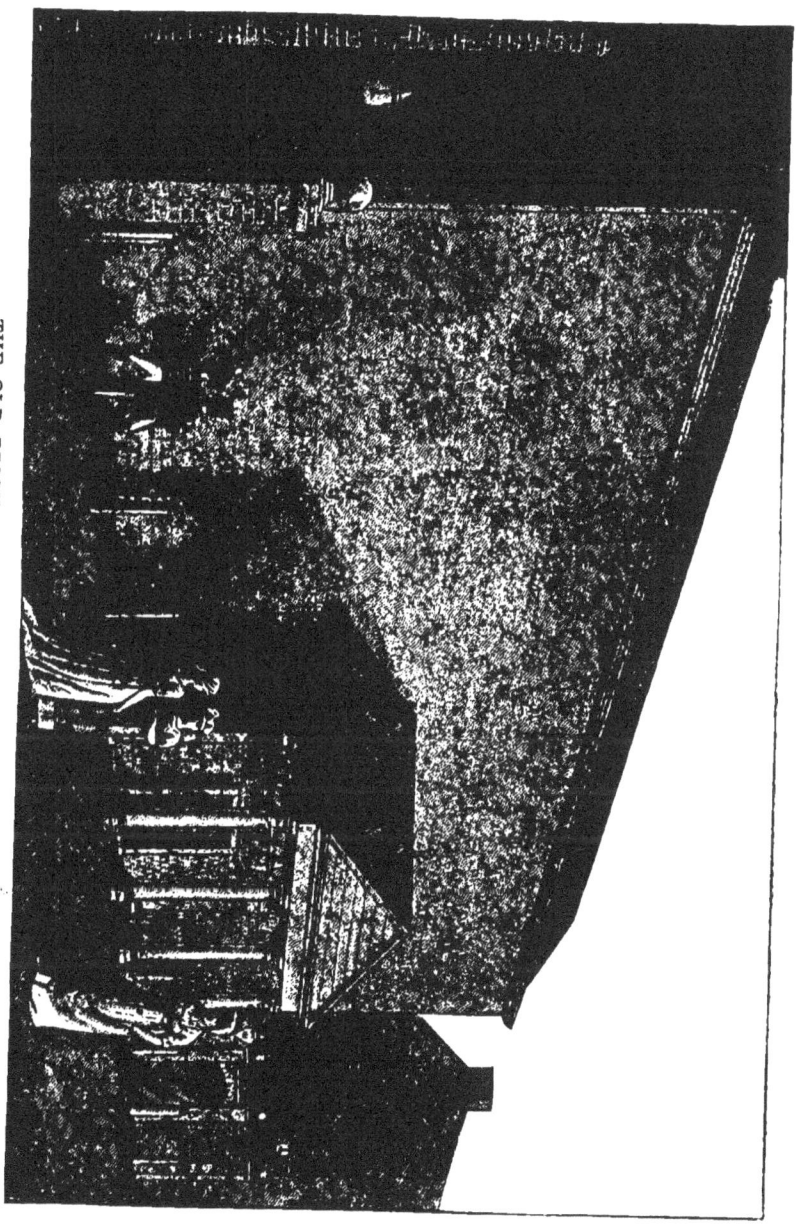

THE OLD BRIGHTON THEATRE.   ERECTED 1790.

discovered and matured. More than that, there is an artistic spirit in the associations of a stock company that gives the work the earnest dignity that befits it. The efforts of the actors have for an end something besides money getting. Then, too, the stock theatre is a potent agent in leading the popular taste. I say 'leading' advisedly, for I believe that the popular taste—the taste of that most valuable element of society which for want of a better term we call the common people—is generally true and good in itself. But it requires direction and guidance. If there should appear a transient tendency toward the meretricious, that tendency must be discouraged. To cater to it by presenting plays and instituting a style of acting not in accord with what is best in art is to do a wrong to those whom we would please. The end of art is not amusement, but improvement and culture."

There seems to be a general clamoring for a new departure in stage productions, not only in the very ranks of the profession, but also in the journals which represent its interest.

One New York dramatic paper recently heads an article "Clear the Temple," which begins by saying: "It must be obvious to the most "careless observer that the world of amusement has for several years "past been in a state of tumult and confusion.

"This applies to all departments, management, authorship and acting. * * * Too much of the spirit of the poolroom, the circus and "the race-course has been introduced in the field of art. That province "which is provided as a sanctuary of retreat from the clamor of the "street and the chicanery of trade, has lost its sequestered and honored "character.

"The realistic jobbers of the out-of-door world have intruded into "the temple of the muses and desecrated its shrine.

"In a word, our theatre, as well as our literature and drama, needs "at this time to have substituted for the wooden idols which now "dominate the living spirits of grace, beauty and eloquence which have "been held as the patron saints of the theatre."

Another dramatic Weekly asks in a headline "Whither are we Drifting," and from its article we quote:

"Why is it that the English-speaking stage has degenerated into an elaboration of such rot as was formerly confined to the London music halls, and is still only found in the Bouffes Parisiennes and Cafes Chantants of Paris? Is there any peculiar twist in the English, and more particularly in the American mind and taste, wherefore the speculator and variety show should have strangled histrionic development? *

* * What was formerly the New York theatre *par excellence* has barely floated during the past five years, because the later management departed from the traditions of the fathers. It attempted to overcome the gathered wisdom of a family of histrions whose *dicta* were always in good taste. * * *

"Verily, we may inquire, Whither are we drifting? when the stage has to stoop to the claptrap advertisements of an English belted Earl, being the treasurer of an indifferent company of not very popular London Minstrels.

"Verily, we can ask, Whither are we drifting? the theatre needs a "Hercules to cleanse the Augean Stables."

Still another article in the same paper on "The Stage of the Future" closes with the following:

"There is no millennium for the American stage in the near future, but there is a fairly good time coming for it; a time when worthy art will have its compensation, and unworthy rot be given to the mob to which it belongs. The weaknesses of the present are natural ones. An uninformed public cannot support a perfect theatre, even if such perfection could grow up in a defective and unfavorable social atmosphere. But the American public is refining itself by experience."

And again another number of one of the above papers contains an editorial under the caption of "Novelties Desired" which closes with these lines:

"The plays that were new to our grandfathers and that have been played ever since more or less, without change, fail to interest the amusement-seekers of to day. Novelty is one of the most powerful attributes of theatrical success and should not be disregarded by our managers. If the theatre can't give the public something new and entertaining, the public will look elsewhere for amusement. A few plays outside of Shakespeare's are always certain of patronage if well presented, but they are very, very few. This is a truth that certain new stars with repertoires will discover to their cost before next season ends."

And still another, one of the most readable dramatic papers of the West, says:

"The fact is that the hectic flush, occasioned by the scramble of all "kinds of people for managerical honors has paled away by frequent "severe losses, and that like every other commercial venture the thea-"trical business has simmered down into one that must depend more "upon brain and experience for success than upon luck. The wild,

"untaimed, tobacco-chewing and whiskey-guzzling managers have
"given place to a more refined class. The hurrah business has, in a
"measure, disappeared, and he who wishes to succeed in the future
"must begin just in the same way as a man of good business qualifica-
"tions would embark in a new enterprise. It is almost degrading to
"be obliged to admit that none of the commercial agencies of the world
"care to give any standing to a theatrical venture of any kind."

Next comes another in an article entitled, "A New Life for the
Theatre," asking: "Is it not possible that some man should arise who,
taking pity on our miserable condition and depressed spirits, created
by the doleful monotony of realistic journalism—cannot some divine
spirit appear among us and put soul and spirit in us.

"Are we to be forever put off with the machine jokes of the funny
men and the automatic gems and insensate horse-laugh of farce-
comedy?"

Are not all the means and appliances of lavish outlay in the equip-
ment of the stage, and wrestling energies employed to grasp attractive
new plays, equal to an effort to drag to the front one man born to be a
light to the stage, a blessing to actors, and become a joy forever to
beaten-down and discouraged audiences?

A well-intentioned paragraphist asserts that the stage is weary of
waiting for the American dramatist of talent and power, and he adds:
"but he will be thrice welcome when he comes."

"Will new men join the ranks of management, or the old managers
turn a new leaf and review the dramatic field from an original point of
view, and not contrive by mere perfunctory repetitions, to still struggle
in the slough of despond? Whatever manager has attempted novelties with a sign of vital life in them and stood by them manfully, has
succeeded. We would like to see more of this heroic administration
of the Theatre, and the wooden idols that have been so persistently
worshipped summarily despatched to the lumber room and scheduled
in the stage vaults as dead fruit."

And not least in this list of wailings and lamentings comes the cry
of another headed: "Is There a Way Out?" beginning: "Let us flee
from the shambles and the charnel house, where nothing is encounter-
ed but slaughter and decay, and enter a temple of peace and good
cheer. Such is the fervent supplication of the dazzled reader as he
throws aside his morning daily, where he has found, in melodorous and
noisome detail, all the crimes, intrigues and shortcomings of the world
in its abnormal spasms for the last four-and-twenty hours.

"The whole country is belittled and vulgarized by the precedence given to crime and its followers. We go further and hand in boquets through the prison bars to convicted murderers and the enemies of society.

"To these offenders and their confreres an ascendancy is given by the preoccupation of the columns of leading publications. Such is the nobility which is daily introduced to our families and made the associates of our most private hours.

"What redress is there to be had—how may we escape this cataclysm which threatens to overwhelm us? Simply that the theatre, which cannot be denied to be a growing power, return to its legitimate province and its own proper work. Let it not attempt to compete with the heavy rush of the slush-flood which has, under the name of Realism, defiled and very nearly disintegrated the drama.

"Restore to us once more representations of man and woman exalted by compassion and exhibit our human nature in all its noblest phases. The true dramatic instinct is surely not to be set aside by adaptations founded on the shifts and devices of characterless offenders against the moral and the civic law.

"In a word, we ask for the stage, the creations of genius and scenes representing a nobler human nature drawn from the resources of the creators of an altogether different and new world. The time has come when the amusement seeker will not be content to step out of the commonplace monotony and cheap incidents of the street to find himself confronted by a repetition of the same under cover of high-priced wearing apparel and a superabundant show of scenic canvass and other flimsy material and mechanical expedients."

And as the last of these cries of despair we condense the following from the pen of one of the ablest of New York critics:

"A REIGN OF RUCK AND ROT ON THE STAGE.—CAPITAL AND INTELLIGENCE TO THE RESCUE.

"Mme —— has been playing here to empty houses. She is one of the most exquisite artists that ever came to America. Round the corner Miss ——, a pet of the rounders, packs the Union Square.

Rot reigns. Up at the —— theatre a comic opera has been produced called "The Little Tycoon," which will give any man of average rational balance the spinal meningitis. I never in all my life saw such innate hogwash scooped by the bucketful from every available cesspool of idiocy. The man that wrote the libretto would have been tarred and feathered in half an hour had he tried to fill the place of a humorist on a penny paper. His lines fall below the candy mottoes of a children's tea-party. His music is borrowed balderdash. And yet large audiences sit the stuff out, and applaud the oldest and most threadbare gags, and grow enthusiastic at the immemorial "ham-fat" that lards the whole thing.

You must come to the conclusion sooner or later that while there is one man in a hundred who can tell an idea from an icicle and doesn't confuse a sonnet with a sardine there are ninety-nine who would quite as readily accept a seven-sheet poster as a fresco of Raphael's.

I suppose you know that the farrago called "The Bunch of Keys" made more money than Henry Irving did during his season. If some innocent lamb should ask you what form of the intellectual drama had been most successful in New York for the last two years, you might run over the names of Booth, Barrett, Davenport, Morris, and Janauschek, and answer "Adonis," the personification of indecency.

At this moment there is not one theatre out of our twenty-four that is presenting serious or worthy work. But there are six of them making an exhibition of ignorant and shapely girls who posturize, giggle rhythmically, and show their legs.

The press, with very few exceptions, treats these shows with the same consideration that it bestows upon the most ambitious and worthy efforts. The louder the exhibition the longer the advertisement, and criticism may be said to have given way to enterprise.

Had Mr. Edwin Booth been possessed of pluck and ambition he could have precipitated this matter.

Just imagine what Booth and Barrett and Joe Jefferson and Lester Wallack might do if it had been given to actors, as it is given to other men, "to pool their issues." This is plain language for a New York critic.

These are naked facts clearly stated. Sound sentiments uttered by nobodies should be more effective for good than heresies promulgated by those in authority; but here are undeniable facts and the healthiest of sentiments put into cold type by those in power and in command.

These are the sound and sincere utterances of the representative members, organs and critics of the dramatic profession. Their acknowledgments and expressions are read principally by actors and the attaches of the theatre and those indirectly connected with the stage and the drama.

That these utterances are boldly flung into the teeth of the theatre by those who receive their main sustenance from the rank and file of the theatrical profession and those whose interests are almost identical with it, is a sign of good augury for the future. The warmth of the expressions indulged in in the above quotations is the result of the earnestness of purpose and intensity of feeling with which matters connected with the drama are nowadays being discussed. Such vehemence is far better than the calmness of indifference.

Many of those at present connected with the theatre insist that its patrons of to-day do not care to be taught anything from the stage. What a mistake this is.

In morals as in life, there is no such thing as *inaction* or *unimpressionableness;* even the most thoughtless auditor *is taught something* whether he cares to be or not. Whatever entertains or amuses him is bound to make an impression upon him and influence his future in spite of himself, and that must be either *for good* or *for evil.*

The fact that the majority of the theatre patrons consists of persons under middle age must not be overlooked. Youth is more impressionable than age. A horror of vice from a sense of its wickedness and its consequences, as it is possible of representation on the stage, is the most effective safeguard for youth against the wickedness of human nature.

The stage speaks in one breath to the cultured and uncultured masses in what ought to be a specially selected language, and the minds and souls of all the listeners are impressed according to the character of the representations. Stage art ought, therefore, never to be prostituted to selfish ends solely. If it is, then it is nothing but duty in those who stand on guard in its own temples to warn against it.

On the other hand, when the drama restricts itself to clearly administering to wholesome recreation and earnest teaching, and when a pure religion shall confine itself to truth and consolation, the struggle between the guardians of both will end, and their work will coincide with each other for the common good.

No man, not a bigot, will question the immense benefit of plays that will check the flow and reduce the volume of the stream of vicious productions which at present revel on the stage of the country.

A Boston Magazine speaking on the "Ethics of the drama," says, "The morality of the stage has come to be as much a matter of concern as an element of popular education as is the morality of the pulpit or the press. Thousands of people sit nightly at our theatres. The

play before them dramatizes the realities of life—its virtues and its
vices, its passions and impulses. Its elements of all that makes life
noble and sacred, or corrupt and degrading, are materialized and placed
in high illumination. The lessons of the stage, whether consciously
or unconsciously given, are peculiarly impressive. The hearer is in a
receptive condition. The "cares that beset the day" are over. He is
mentally open to suggestion, and is easily borne on with the mysterious
magnetism of the hour. If the drama is one intrinsically noble, ideally
true, the inner-man receives a distinct moral impulse. The reverse
also may be true. Of late there has been no little controversy among
theatre managers of New York regarding the morality of the stage.
A prominent one, as we have shown in the beginning, expressed his
opinion that the ballet was an affair of gross immorality.

An actor, who, as an artist and a keen observer of life, is entitled
to a two-fold consideration, believes that dramatic art is deteriorating;
that the theatres cater to the eye rather than to the mind, and that
finance and art are opposing factors in the drama. He sees that the
moral tone of the plays is lower than formerly, and that many entertainments are degrading. The gentleman here touches a wholesome,
moral truth.

While the dramatization of life must present the vices as well as
the virtues of character, but there is no need that it should present the
indecencies.

Shakespeare's men and women image every quality and tendency
of human life. Vice, treason, corruption and their terrible results are
seen side by side with virtue, purity, patriotism and exaltation, but the
lesson impressed is wholly noble.

This cannot be said of new plays now on the stage. Their degradation is of a nature that renders their influence, one leading to moral
decadence, to an undermining of character, and is one calculated to
lessen the swift discrimination between virtue and vice.

Dramatic art is based on the differences of human character; life's
intercourse is a game between superiors and inferiors. Every being
is stirred by a desire to rise above those about him and to make this
apparent to them. Among men and women of low sensibility, more
deference is paid to dress and title than to form and bearing. Descent
and station are placed above merit and worth. Quiet actions are
crowded aside by shows and pretensions. Wealth is esteemed above
character. This fills the world with confusion, wickedness and
misery.

No two men can be exactly alike; without inequality there would be unbroken monotony. The fair struggle for superiority is the divine method of enchanting us with the world. But all this struggle must have a reasonable limit.

Life would be an unmixed good, were it not for the vices of peculation, of false pretense, of fraud, envy and tyranny. If we regarded one another with reverence, friendship and kindness the difference in human character would be the chief elements of life's delight. But it is otherwise, and this is cause for regret.

The dramatic spirit freely enters the soul. The genuine temper of this art, separated from its depraved usages of to-day, can teach us more effectively than any other medium to help those beneath us, to love the good and the true around us. The strong and the cunning would not then take such undue advantages of the weak, unsophisticated and honest, nor would they then hold the masses in subjection by fraud and fear.

Life might become a mutual teaching and blessing, a learning and following, a giving and taking of all good things in justice and love, and without violence.

There are a certain select few in whom the secrets and powers of human nature are revealed to a greater extent than in others. In their hands the keys of power are lodged, and mankind pays tribute to them for the benefits they claim to bestow. If they, in all cases, disinterestedly used their power to free, enlighten and strengthen other men, to educate, ennoble and enrich them from their stores of knowledge and skill, the world would be far better to-day than it is.

But the majority of these have ever used their knowledge, skill and power, only to secure special advantages to themselves, and corrupt their surroundings instead of bettering them. Therefore the greedy struggles, the unequal strifes, the grinding poverty of body and soul, and the misery and the crimes of the world continue to increase from day to day in greater proportions than the natural increase of living humanity.

How can this fatal spell be broken? How can rugged honesty, truth, courage and virtue be made to prevail? It can only be brought about by an increased spirit of sympathy for truth and right. This must be made the great problem of the home, of the school, of the press, of the pulpit, and last, though by no means least, of the theatre. Not one of these can afford to scorn, nay, each must have the proper help of the other.

The theatre, in order to escape from its tawdry frivolity of to-day and take its proper place among the other factors of reform must take up the academic spirit of earnest instruction and add to what it already possesses, moral earnestness. When the theatre does this then all the other factors must yield to it,—to the drama and to its interpreters of genius and experience,—the palm for the completeness with which they pierce the secrecy of human nature and command its manifestations while they warn from the unworthy with fear and loathing, and draw to the excellent with admiration and love.

This is contagious education disguised in entertainment; earnest improvement, concealed in play; and edification masked in recreation; this is the way to break the fatal spell.

We cry with one of the critics quoted in the early part of this article, "Clear the Temple."

There is only one way out of this ruck. If the theatre is of any educational value, or is worth preserving, there is but one way to hold it in its best estate against this deluge of sensuality and frivolity, and that way is for capital and intelligence to come to its rescue. When we think of what capital has done, for opera we wonder why some of the millionaires do not rescue the drama. One of the richest men in New York said last winter at the Metropolitan Opera House: "We want a National theatre, where only the best players and best plays can be seen, and it will come. It must not be at the mercy of popular moods. Its organization and character must guarantee excellence, and then the great conservative classes will be drawn to it. It's in the air," he said, "and it will come."

The sun's darkest setting is followed by its rising. Death is succeeded by birth. What will the morrow bring? A destructive storm or a bright and reviving orb? What will the new birth be? A monstrocity or a more perfect being than ever? Wait and hope.

THE RIGHT TO HISS.

The following is clipped from a recent issue of a New York Weekly:

TO HISS OR NOT TO HISS.

This mooted question seems to be agitating both the theatrical community and the public which pays its way into the theatre.

There is no question but the person who pays the box office price to enter a theatre has the inalienable right to a performance for the money paid, and, for that matter, to a good performance, too: but here that right ceases, and if one person or a combination of persons in an auditorium, feeling that they are not getting the worth of their money, commit an act which tends to provoke a breach of the peace, it is the bounden duty of the authorities to interfere by arrest.

Suppose a person entered a large restaurant crowded with people, and because the article served was not to the liking of the purchaser would he dare show his disrespect and disregard for the same in the manner shown by disapprobation in a theatre? Assuredly not.

Therefore, say we, and so says the law, to hiss is to act disorderly. To act disorderly in a public place is a breach of the public peace, and he who thus offends is as culpable as he who in his cups in the street is annoying to the passer-by, and who, when arraigned before a magistrate, is put under bonds or fined for thus violating the law.

Is it too severe to style this article "the height of idiocy?" I think not. Mr. Joseph Knight, one of the ablest dramatic critics England has had of late years, in speaking of hissing says: "I am anxious to preserve in the public, which I hold to be the true guardian of the stage, a healthy sentiment. In order to do this I would maintain its right within reasonable limits to express disapproval. I hold that the custom of pronouncing condemnation besides encouraging a healthy interest in the drama, is beneficial to actors and managers."

Mr. Frank Marshall, another English authority, says: "I am the very last person to dispute the right of every spectator at a theater to express disapprobation. There can be no doubt that if an audience is allowed to applaud it should also be allowed to hiss."

Mr. Palgrave Simpson, still another authority, and a dramatist at

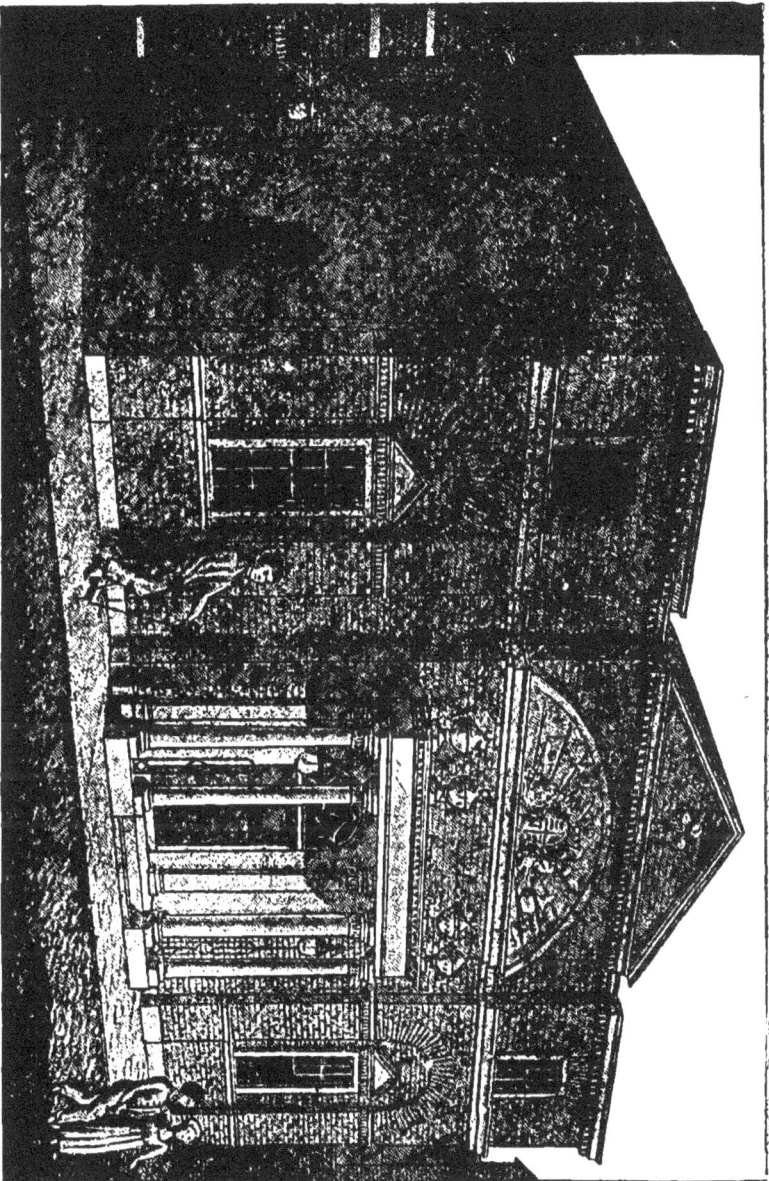

THEATRE AT NEWCASTLE. ERECTED 1789.

that, argues: "Far be it from any real lover of the drama to call for the entire suppression of the long-established manner of displaying dissatisfaction. But the right of hissing ought certainly only to be exercised at proper times and without tumult."

Another eminent critic in an English dramatic monthly says: "A person who hisses has no more right to be disturbed than one who applauds, provided that by hissing he does not irritate or annoy the great body of the audience. Let us have free judgment by all means. When a play is shown to be bad let it be hissed. When an actor plays the fool and takes liberties let him be brought up suddenly with the whip that the audience holds in reserve."

A dozen or more authorities in the same strain could be cited if there were really any doubt as to the rights of the patrons as the recognized censors of the productions of the stage.

To compare a restaurant in this connection with the theatre is certainly "the height of idiocy." Does the patron of the restaurant applaud and stamp his feet when he finds his viands palatable? If the meat is not sufficiently well cooked he calls for such as is, and it is cheerfully exchanged. The patron of the theatre pays for his ticket in advance. The presumption is that he has not yet seen the play or has not heard a certain company of actors in that particular play. If he is pleased with both, he is permitted to demonstrate his approval; if he is displeased with either, who can dispute his right to give recognized signs of his displeasure, as we have never known of a rule with managers to refund the price of admission or even exchange the tickets for another performance, under the latter condition of things.

The *right* to hiss has ever been admitted, even by actors and authors, during a long course of years. Colley Cibber complained in his time of its severity. He did not question the right of the audience to hiss. He only protested against its indiscriminate and too violent exercise.

It was not until the occurrence of quite a riot at Covent Garden, in 1773, when an attempt was made to drive the actor Macklin off the stage, that any legal decision was rendered on the subject. It was held that as the theatre was open for the reception and entertainment of those who paid for their admission, the audience had a right to applaud, condemn, and even reject any of the performers; but if any conspiracy was formed before-hand to effect the condemnation or rejection of plays or players, redress was obtainable by an action at law. Lord Mansfield took occasion to say that the right of hissing or applauding was "an unalterable right," but that there was a great difference between expressing the natural sensations of the mind as they arose on what was seen and heard, and the execution of a preconcerted design not only to hiss but to create a disturbance. The right to hiss became again the subject of a legal decision in the case of Clifford vs. Braadon, about 1810, at the time of the famous "O. P." riots at Covent Garden, without any departure, however, from the precedent established in Macklin's case.

Of late years there has been little question concerning *the right* to hiss. In August, 1880, an auditor hissed in a London music hall because a child only five years old was allowed to sing a song on the stage at eleven o'clock at night. The magistrate expressed himself, that any person going to a place of public entertainment had a right to express an opinion of the value of the exhibition, and fined the defendant-manager 20s. and cost for compelling, with but little violence, the complainant-auditor to leave the hall. The Parisian play goers have never surrendered the right to hiss a bad performance. The French law, while recognizing the right of the *paying* spectator to hiss if he is disappointed in the play or the acting will not allow any cabal or conspiracy, and forbids any boisterous or disturbing demonstration except while the curtain is up. As soon as it is down everything must be decorum.

That American audiences *do not* make better use of this *right* is only to be regretted. There certainly seems to be no more justice in interfering with the rights of an auditor who hisses than with those of one who applauds. Nay, injudicious and indiscriminate applause is more likely to disturb the enjoyment of others and to destroy the illusion than hissing. No form of applause but what is certainly more noisy than mere hissing. There are moments during almost any evening's entertainment when many an undemonstrative listener, if he could do it peacably, without disturbing his quiet neighbor on one side, would cheerfully take his exuberant neighbor on the other, and lift him bodily into the middle of the street for injudiciously applauding.

If the right to hiss were as freely exercised as it should be in American theatres, there would be fewer auditors annoyed by it than there are now by indiscriminate applause, and we should have to-day a purer drama and be spared the affliction of much bad acting.

Since the publication of the foregoing article in "Music and Drama," the following letter from a prominent English actor, not unknown in this country from his occupying the leading position under Mr. Henry

Irving in his American tour, has appeared in the *London Era*. It was prompted by the severe treatment a new play had just then received at a prominent London theatre. As it bears directly on the main subject of the above article the letter is herewith given in full, with the comments of another correspondent attached:

To the Editor of the Era:

SIR—In the recent controversy which has taken place with regard to the conduct of "first night audiences" at London theatres a great deal of opprobrium and coarse abuse has been showered on a class for whom I, as an actor, have a great respect, and as silence is generally taken to signify assent I should like to put upon record my entire *dissent* from the abuse which has been heaped upon "first-nighters."

To read many of the letters on this subject one would suppose that this section of the playgoing public was composed of the dregs of society. Now, I have acted in a great many theatres and on a great many first nights. I claim to know something about London and provincial audiences, and I fearlessly assert that the occupants of the pit, who make it a rule to attend first nights, are the most intelligent judges to be found amongst those who honour the theatre with their support. They are a body of gentlemen who love the drama for the drama's sake. They have studied their subject, with them "the play's the thing;" they are not to be acted upon by any outside influences; they come prepared to express an honest opinion, to applaud that which they think good and to condemn that which they think bad; they are a fearless body, and their presence has a most salutary effect upon both actors and upon managers ; and I feel sure that a great deal of the care and attention bestowed upon theatrical performances nowadays is due to the wholesome respect which actors and managers have for this class of playgoers, who have lately been so freely abused.

A good deal has been said about organized opposition. I for one do not believe in the existence of anything of the kind, but I do believe in original approbation, and I know there have been theatres in London which on a first night have been packed (as far as possible) with the friends of the management, who were expected to applaud both in season and out of season, and who, by their noisy approval, very often provoked the counter demonstration of those who came to judge on their merits, both the play and the players. Managers and actors should bear in mind that the only real judges of their work are the paying public, and from their judgment there is no appeal, nor, singular to relate, is there any inclination to appeal when the judgment is a favorable one.

Why, then, in the name of all that's logical, should there be such an outcry when the decision is adverse? I maintain that the public have a perfect right to condemn a play, and we all know that if a play or the acting be outrageously bad it is certain to provoke outrageous comment, and I think it is absurd to condemn a whole class because some few members of its body have let their zeal outrun their discretion. Authors and actors know perfectly well when they bid for popular favour that they run the risk of incurring popular condemnation, and if they fear the ordeal they had better keep off the stage altogether, and not· set up a whining cry when the public assert their undoubted right of pronouncing an adverse judgment upon their efforts.

It is all very well to claim the indulgence due to ladies and gentlemen, but artists should remember that they are actors and actresses when they are on the boards, and if they wish to be treated as ladies and gentlemen only they had better remain in that privacy with which the public will not interfere, and where they will be free alike from public applause and public censure.

For my part, I frankly confess that I value highly the applause of the first-nighter. I fearlessly acknowledge his right to hiss equally with his right to applaud, and if, in the exercise of his judgment, he should think right to hiss me, I shall not flinch from his verdict, but I shall set myself seriously to examine my shortcomings, and endeavour, by hard work, to convert an adverse decision into a favourable one.

I think that all connected with the theatre are indebted to these intelligent critics, and it will be a bad day for the drama when it excites so languid an interest in the public mind as to decrease the number of the enthusiastic playgoers who form the much-vilified first-nighters.   I am, Sir, your obedient servant,

X.

Adelphi Theatre, January 19th, 1886.

To the Editor of the Era:

SIR—If all professionals were as clear-headed, right-minded, and courageous as Mr. X. has shown himself to be in his common-sense letter which appeared in your last issue, there would be less friction than there is between the stage and the public, less hysterical abuse on the one part, and less feeling of rankling on the other.

Mr. X. puts the matter so clearly that, if it were not that many of his brother and sister artists and their toadies were not blinded by prejudice and conceit, his letter would end this everlasting controversy.

If bad plays and incompetent players were not hissed there would soon be no room for good plays and competent players on the stage. Foolishness is always compared with talent in the proportion of ten to one, and if the public (which on first nights is represented solely by the gallery and pit) were the open-mouth fools that some critics and players would have them be, and swallowed what was put before them without daring to think for themselves, good plays. and players would be at a discount, as managers could get rubbish at one-tenth the present cost, and it would answer their purposes just as well. The fact is, good plays and players need fear no independent judgment; it is the bad that always cry out.

Mr. X. will not be thanked by his short-sighted companions, but he has earned the thanks of the whole play-going community by his outspoken and manly remarks.

I am, Sir, yours obediently,   Y.

London, January 26th, 1886.

THEATRE ROYAL, LIVERPOOL.   ERECTED 1772.

PRECHER OR CLOWN.

More than sufficient time has elapsed since their departure, so that the question as to the permanent effect of the work of the two revivalists, Jones and Small, is certainly now a pertinent one. If religious workers are to employ such outside assistance and expend large sums of money for it, it is surely no more than fair to those who contribute the funds, to insist upon a close scrutiny of the alleged benefits resulting from the labors of pretended reformers.

In the accounts of the revival work, both in Cincinnati and here, the converts were said to number thousands. Judging by the extravagant assertions of both the secular and religious press, one might suppose that the churches were being thronged in both cities with new members and that a moral revolution was at hand.

These two men came at the request of several of our leading churches. They had the benefit of more free advertising than a theatrical manager could secure at a thousand dollars a week. What have they accomplished now that the excitement has died away? What has become of the thousands of men and women converted in the great revival meetings of these two great apostles? With the exception of Moody no religious speakers have been able to call together such enthusiastic crowds. If they have not been able to rescue at least hundreds from the gutter, the gambling hells, the gin mills, or the road to the prison, their work has been in vain from an outside point of view, for then even their temporary converts of a light calibre have surely gone back to their old ruts and are living the same dishonorable lives as heretofore.

If the effect of the exhorters work is not felt in the houses of the Lord by an increase of membership, of what benefit to religion can their work be claimed to be more than any other movement to advance abstract theories of honesty and right. Lecturing to the people against the non-payment of debts and against intemperance, against gambling and against extravagance in dress, can be carried on with equal force by the society of ethical culture, by the Tom Payne association, and finally far more effectively and with more permanent benefit, in the theatre by good plays.

"It is fruit-bearing that tells the growth of the church," says Mr. Beecher.

The church is supposed to gain in permanent followers by the work of religious revivalists. If that is not clearly the result of their labors—and investigation in Cincinnati and here in Chicago, has shown that such is not the case—then it cannot be claimed that these two men have accomplished anything worth the powder expended.

Since about all the use that Jones and Small had for church-organizations and the regular ministers of the gospel, was to hold them up to censure and to ridicule them, it will require better evidence than that heretofore adduced to show what the church has gained by getting down to their level and encouraging the style which was their specialty.

In Baltimore, where they were in May last, a sensation has been created by a card published by the Rev. W. Kirkus, a leading Protestant Episcopal clergyman. He writes:

I think it time to protest against the gross and insolent abuse which these gentlemen have thought proper in the presence of thousands of people to offer to a very large number of our Baltimore citizens. And when it is publicly asserted that all these ladies who took part in the kirmes or in the charity ball, or who play whist with their tired husbands, or take part in progressive euchre, or who dance, are "hugging to music," are emissaries of the Devil, are helping their husbands and families to hell, I think it time to ask who gave to the people who make these charges the right to sit in the judgment seat of the Eternal and condemn to hellfire hundreds of the purest, most noble, most self-sacrificing women on the face of the earth?

We are not accustomed here in Baltimore to hear the ladies of Baltimore condemned for gross vice without accusers, or trial, or jury, by a couple of irresponsible people who know nothing about them. As one of the clergy of Baltimore, I beg to say that these women, so ruthlesly slandered, are our personal friends, are of spotless reputation, and are among our best workers, are welcomed by us to the holy Eucharist, and are, at the very least, far above suspicion of impurity and ungodliness as the men who so wickedly and insolently abuse them.

Is it not now apparent to the naked eye that their—at best—humorous style, which was certainly of a very low order, simply drew together thousands of mere entertainment-seekers, people who can never be induced to permanently connect themselves with the regular church, men and women who do not regard religion as at all essential to happiness in this world, yet all of whom may stand sorely in need of substanstial reformation, but very few of which they have drawn to a more religious life. The entire population of this city is clearly traveling the same road as it was, before Jones and Small appeared here.

An incident which shows the estimate placed upon their work in this article to be a correct one, and which shows that the thousands who listened to them were not lost beyond redemption, and might possibly be influenced for the better by another factor altogether, occurred on the occasion of their last meeting at which no less than 10,000 souls were present. It is taken from a report in a daily paper, and reads:

The evening audience was enthusiastic, and when a young woman played "Sweet By-and-by" on a cornet, an encore was demanded, and the choir was obliged to sing to stop the noise. Only a few of the vast crowd seemed to note the incongruity of an encore in a religious service. There were no recalls when a vigorous prayer was offered.

Does not this incident prove that the work of these two expensive revivalists in the interest of *real* religion, is only about on a par with that of the present day clown of the stage in the interest of the *real* drama. They simply catch the superficial and thoughtless for the brief hour of their exhibition.

The revival work of Jones and Small in the church does no more deserve to be ranked with the labors of a Beecher, a Collier, a Swing, a Thomas, and ever so many lesser lights—than do the exhibitions of the clowns on the stage deserve to be mentioned in the same breath with the sublime acting of a Forest, a Salvini, a Booth, a Cushman or a Janauchek. Mountebanks "may make the unskillful laugh, but can only make the judicious grieve." They can not permanently raise their hearers to better thoughts, nor to a purer life. Jones and Small can not pose as reformers. Reform must be accomplished by other means and other men.

A SOCIAL REVOLUTION.

HOW TO INAUGURATE IT—A NEW CLASS OF PATRONAGE FOR THE
THEATRE—THEATRICAL FASHIONS.

The atheistic tendency of instruction in our schools can not be gainsaid. One can read it between the lines of the text books of all nondenominational schools and institutions, none of which directly acknowledge the existence of an all-wise creator. Even christian classics are displaced by works of science based on atheism.

If this, in the estimation of true believers, opens the way to moral destruction, how can the thousands of our rising generation be rescued from this inevitable end. It certainly can not be done by the church alone, while its right to recognition and existence is denied in the early training of those whom it seeks to save.

It can, however, unquestionably be successfully inaugurated by the theatre if its power and influence is properly directed and utilized. The church, of course, can greatly assist in such an inauguration, and once started all progress will be comparatively easy.

Many minds, however, whose opinions with reference to other subjects we are bound to respect, seem to be utterly adrift, if not hopelessly in error, as to the legitimate sphere and the power for good of the drama and the theatre proper.

In a number of articles heretofore contributed to "Music and Drama" and particularly the one entitled "The Church and the Theatre," much has been said on this subject.

It is to be hoped that the thoughtful reader, who feels an interest in the welfare of his kind, has found these unpretentious efforts attractive and instructive.

Of course, if serious results are to be attained by means of the stage, serious work has to be done for and by it.

THE THEATRE AT BIRMINGHAM.   ERECTED 1795.

To arouse a lasting interest in a better class of dramatic productions on the stage of this country, and to, at least partially, crowd out the usurping trash, is not easily accomplished. It will not only require plays specially prepared for this purpose, but also abler critics with broader views and more honesty of purpose, a large number of accomplished and enthusiastic stage artists, a more elevated taste amongst regular theatre-goers, but above all an extensive recruiting for an entirely new class of patronage which now studiously denies any good to the theatre and with which the patronizing of plays for this purpose must first be made a matter of fashion, if not a matter of principle.

Society has always been full of tyrannical errors and prejudices to which it clings with great stubbornness, and against which even those liberally inclined, dislike to speak and labor openly and boldly. Goethe, however, said that unwelcome convictions courageously uttered are like the pawns first moved on the chess board; they might meet with stubborn opposition, but they inaugurated a game which could be ultimately won.

Tastes and fashions in dramatic exhibitions have been almost as varied from their earliest period as the fashions in dress. That which was popular in one age became almost obsolete in the next, and the stage is a very ancient institution. Although its fashions, so to speak, changed, as an institution it was always popular.

Even among the most remote Chinese traditions, the theatre holds a very early and most conspicuous place. In ancient Greece the profession was accounted honorable; in Rome it was well requited; in Athens the theatre was a temple in which the audience were taught how the will, not only of men, but of gods, must necessarily submit, to the irresistible force of destiny. It formed a portion of the religion of the state, its religious character in Greece being specially supported, on behalf of the audience, by the ever sagacious, moral, and pious chorus.

Lyric tragedy with its choruses was much in vogue before the age of Thespis, but a spoken tragedy dates from that period alone, which was about five centuries earlier than the Christian era. Roscius, the popular comedian, contemporary with Cicero, was elevated by Sulla, the famous Roman general, to the equestrian dignity, and with Aesopus, the tragedian, enjoyed the friendship of Tully, the third king of Rome, and his friends.

It surely was the fashion when Cæsar induced Decius Saberius, an author of knightly rank, to appear on the stage in one of his own pieces.

5

The christian fathers afterwards leveled their denunciations against that stage only which was given up to scandalous exhibitions, whereas they approved a "well-trod stage."

The minds and hearts of England were ever open to dramatic impressions. The Druidical rites were popular because they contained the elements of dramatic spectacle. In the Pagan-Saxon era dialogue actors became the fashion. When the period of Christianity succeeded, its professors and teachers took of the evil epoch, that which best suited their purposes. They dramatized the incidents of the lives of the saints in narrative dialogue or in song. The men who best performed the united offices of missionary and actor in castle hall, before farm house fires, on the bridges and in the market places, were the most popular preachers, among whom St. Anhelm was the greatest of his time.

The mixture of the sacred and the profane in the early dialogues and dramas, prevailed for a long time until the profane superabounded, when the higher church authorities found it necessary to look to it. The monotony of monastic life had caused the wandering gleemen with their frivolous songs to be too popular within the monastery circles. These very songs were mostly written by the monks themselves.

The more serious of them then thought it wise to prohibit these indulgences. The council of Clovershoe and decrees bearing the king's mark, ordained that actors should no longer have access to the monasteries. About this time, the year 1119, one Geoffrey, a monk, rented a house at Silvester Daggerwood, where he had a regular drama represented, which had St. Katherine for a heroine and her whole life for a subject. This managing monk soon after withdrew from the profession upon the destruction by fire of this, one of the earliest of English theatres, and then retired again to his cell at St. Albans to find a home for the remainder of his days.

Then a course of plays, illustrating scripture and the sufferings of martyrs—moralities—in which the vices were in antagonism to the virtues, rose to popularity, and we finally arrive in England at legitimate tragedy and comedy. Up to this time the church as regularly employed the stage for moral and even religious ends, as the old heathen governments did, when they made festivals the means of maintaining a religious feeling among the people.

The present day believers in a pure faith therefore make a great mistake when they refuse to endorse or advocate the serious illustration of biblical subjects by dramatic exhibitions through which the thoughts of an audience may be elevated to a level with the subject.

In this regard history must be forced to repeat itself. The world can learn none too soon that of all human folly, religious short-sightedness—born of selfishness and possibly prompted by a fear of loosing entirely its constantly waning hold upon a narrow circle—is the worst obstruction to a true religion and its advancement. If christians in early history were able to view with pleasure the miracle-plays in which the gravest truths of the gospel were dramatically represented, why should such an association of subjects, seriously treated, now cause irreverent familiarity on the stage any more than on canvass, in marble or through the medium of music.

The popularity of the theatre properly used, is the only way to check the populace in its rabid rush down the precipice of moral degradation.

If performances of such a character could be made fashionable and popular to-day, the millions who now ignore the church and its teachings, might again be made familiar with biblical history, the very foundation of religion, which at present they are not. It may be safely asserted that since, by slow degrees the teaching of christianity has been eliminated from all our state schools, the Bible is read less than any historical book in print, and this in the face of the fact that religion, or at least biblical history, is taught in the public schools of almost every other portion of the world.

In connection with this subject it must be interesting to mention here, that a London journal recently commenced the publication of a series of opinions from English men and women of note as to the best books to be recommended for reading by the great body of the people. Sir John Lubbock having first submitted to the journal in question a list of a hundred books among which the Bible did not appear, the editor, among other letters received the following:

Sir: In reply to your inquiry I am directed by Mr. Chamberlain to say that he does not think he could greatly improve the list of books already submitted by Sir John Lubbock. He would, however, inquire whether it is by accident or design that the Bible has been omitted. I am, yours obediently,

WILLIAM WOODINGS.

MR. HENRY IRVING.

My Dear Sir: In reply to your courteous request I should say: Before a hundred books commend me first to the study of two—the Bible and Shakspeare.

Obediently yours,

HENRY IRVING.

The reading of the Bible, however, is not fashionable at present.

As to fashion in other spheres in life the "Virginia Law Journal" in its May number had a well prepared article, apropos to this entire subject under the somewhat anomalous title of "Judicial Fashions," taking the ground that even the judiciary are not removed from those epidemic influences in life, which at times take possession of the human mind and "make fashionable" human action in every day affairs. It says among other pertinent truths:

"A tendency to run away with things seems to be a characteristic of the human mind. By some law of conscious or unconscious imitation, fashions are set in dress, in manners, in the sports of children, in the amusements of youth, in the habits of mature age. When once a thing is started, the body of the community falls into line, and the new mode has its day, until some fresher fancy supersedes it.

"This law of imitation pervades even the graver fields of thought. Special aspects of scientific speculation, theories more or less novel, or old ones in a new dress, have their day, and run their course like the cut of a coat, or the shape of a bonnet. This tendency is very noticable in medical practice, and in the lines of theological thought and discussion. Even on the bench we find it holding sway with learned and experienced judges, engaged in the most practical of human professions."

As the "Law Journal" truly says here, "when once a thing is started"—properly started, of course, with a well worked boom, as the street phrase now has it,—"the body of the community falls into line."

If the thing—the idea or proposition—to be started is in proper season, has reason and a good purpose, has the elements of popularity —in fact of fashion—in it, so much the better. It will then be sure of success and of profit to the starter, if profit is essential for its beneficial continuance. The fact that profit may possibly be the prime object of the starter, will of itself, in no way lessen the corrective value of the thing, if it be otherwise worthy and good in its effect.

The receptive condition of society at the time of the "start" and the general surroundings in which the start is made always largely govern its success. The American people are "great" on "falling into line." Yesterday it was a walking-match or a skating rink, to-day it is the dime museum or tobogganing, to-morrow it may be a Jones and Small or—a Bible-play.

In connection with no enterprises is it so easy to make a thing fashionable as it is in those of the amusements of a people. True, there are many failures of theatrical ventures on record within the last few years. These, however, are really attributable to the senseless over-doing of a thing already started, rather than to any errors of judgment in the first start of a new one.

Any manager or actor who will boldly carve out for himself, a path in the direction indicated, or any individual or body of well-meaning moralists who shall encourage, or inaugurate, what will lead to a complete change of front on the part of the church in conjunction with the theatre, for the purpose of instilling the sentiments of a pure faith and the doctrines and moral precepts of christianity into their fellow-beings, will surely reap an everlasting reward in the blessings, from the thoughtful people of their country in the near future. Whom the school refuses to instruct, and the church can not reach, the theatre may.

ILLUSTRATIONS.

OLD LONDON THEATRES.

The "Paris Garden Theatre" was erected prior to 1544, under the reign of King Henry the VIII. It derived its name from Robert de Paris who had a house and grounds there in the reign of Richard the II. When first built it was used solely for "Bear-baiting," but it was occasionally employed as a theatre for dramatic representations as early as 1592, and it was re-built into a regular playhouse, similar to the "Swan Theatre" on the Bankside, after the burning of the "Globe theatre" in the latter part of the year 1613, and used as a regular theatre up to 1647, it having by that time come into possession of the crown.

The "Globe Theatre" was built and opened in 1504 according to a bond entered into by Richard Burbage, the actor, dated Dec. 20, 1593. The building was destroyed by fire on St. Peter's day, June 29th, 1613, upon which occasion Ben Jonson the poet was present. It was rebuilt in the following spring "in far fairer manner than before," but pulled down in 1647, and not heard of again after the Restoration. Shakespeare was at one time part owner of this theatre.

The "Fortune Theatre" was erected in Golden or Golding Lane in the Parish of St. Giles, Cripplegate, in 1599. According to the contract between Henslow and Alleyn, the managers, and Peter Streete the builder, the outer dimensions were eighty feet each way. It had three tiers and was thirty-two feet high. Its general arrangements and construction inside, was similar to the "Globe," which had also been erected by Streete, and was under Henslowe and Alleyns management at that time. The house was consumed by fire in December, 1621, and was not again re-built until 1623, and finally pulled down in 1661.

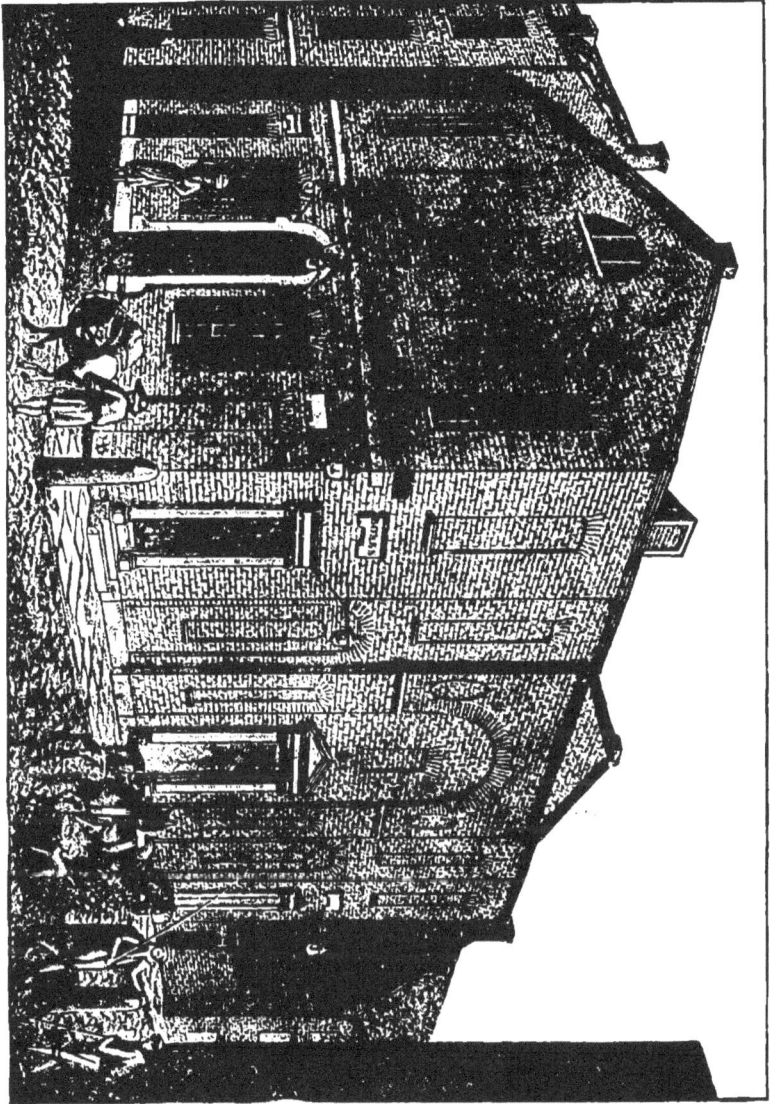

THEATRE ROYAL, MANCHESTER. ERECTED 1774.

ENGLISH PROVINCIAL THEATRES A HUNDRED YEARS AGO.

In the picture of the old Bath Theatre it will be sufficient to point out that the first door is the avenue leading to the stage, the second to the galleries, and the third to the pit. The fourth was made in 1800 for the convenience of entering the boxes, it being found that two chairs were sufficient to block up the regular entrance. The Windsor Theatre was built in 1703; the Portsmouth Theatre in 1761.

The old Brighton Theatre, in Duke Street, was erected in 1790. The Newcastle Theatre, in Mosely Street, was opened with the comedy of *The Way to Keep Him*, in 1789. The Theatre Royal, Liverpool, in Williamson Square, was opened on June 5, 1772, with a prologue written by the Elder George Coleman. The Birmingham Theatre, built on the ground occupied by a previous edifice destroyed by fire, was opened by Mr. Macready on the 18th of June, 1795. The Manchester Theatre Royal here represented, was opened with *Othello* on Whit Monday, 1774.

THE NEW OPERA HOUSE IN PARIS.

The erection of "The National Academy of Music," which is the official title of what all Paris calls simply "The Opera" was begun in July 1862, but the building was not completed until the end of the year 1874. The engraving which serves as a frontispiece represents the front elevation. Mons. Charles Garnier, the architect, not only designed the entire building but he also lived to complete the entire structure, which covers an area of 2¾ acres and cost $7,400,000. In 1864 the side walls were completed. On August 15, 1867, the front scaffolding was removed and the front of Mons. Garnier's work was revealed for the first time. During the war with Prussia the building was used for a hospital and a storehouse, and during the time of the Siege of Paris the roof was used as a signal station. In the latter part of 1874 the building was completed and turned over to the management. It is the most prominent monument which France has erected and the most magnificent theatre in the world to house the union of music and the drama, its "foyer" or crush room alone being 179 feet long, 43 feet broad and 59 feet high. Its auditorium has seats for 2,000 people.

A MIRACLE-PLAY AT METZ IN 1440.

The sun of a lovely autumn day in 1440 has just gone down beyond the "Porte Serpenoise" of the then self-styled "noble cité,"—of the ancient and celebrated free city of Metz—free up to 1648 when it had to succumb to France. In this illustration we see the magnificent cathedral begun in the 13th century, and the neighboring monastry of St. Arnulf surrounded by its glass works and tanneries. Upon the platform or stage—erected specially for the presentation of plays—in front of the main entrances, they are just going through the last scenes of the miracle—or Christ-play, the first scene of which was the birth of Christ. The group to the left on the stage,—beyond which we see the corner of an altar representing "Bethlehem"—is the Holy Family passing through the rich fields of Egypt to Nazareth, which place is indicated by the sign "Nazareth" over the arched door to the left of the throne. Herod upon his throne in the center—to the right of which we find the sign "Jerusalem" over the door—is being dragged away by the fiends of darkness, who carry him bodily to the infernal regions represented by the opened jaws of the monster on the right, high beyond which rises the prison, surmounted by a fantastic monster.

Most prominent among the spectators is the historically celebrated Sir Nicole Louve, commander of the city, and his family. The entire representation is at his expense to celebrate his victory over Sir Robert de Commercy of Lorraine. In the right hand corner stands Sir Nicole in his official robes and high black hat, the insignia of his office; near and almost hidden in front of him, visible only by the horns of her head-dress protruding over his shoulder and over the hat of his charming neighbor, sits Lady Claudia, his wife. The charming neighbor at his elbow is Lady Isabelle, his eldest daughter, who has just closed the text book of the play before her and is for the moment directing the attention of an unseen lady friend near her, to some special point of the performance. At the extreme left stands the brave young cavalier, Sir Harry de Baudoche, the favorite suitor for the hand of Lady Isabelle, which he claims as a reward for his gallant conduct in the defence of the city. The actors upon this memorable occasion are some of the most aristocratic young men of this highly aristocratic city.

www.ingramcontent.com/pod-product-compliance
Lightning Source LLC
Chambersburg PA
CBHW032248080426
42735CB00008B/1056